Collaborating with High Schools

Janet E. Lieberman, *Editor*
LaGuardia Community College

NEW DIRECTIONS FOR COMMUNITY COLLEGES
ARTHUR M. COHEN, *Editor-in-Chief*
FLORENCE B. BRAWER, *Associate Editor*

Number 63, Fall 1988

Paperback sourcebooks in
The Jossey-Bass Higher Education Series

Jossey-Bass Inc., Publishers
San Francisco • London

Janet E. Lieberman (ed.).
Collaborating with High Schools.
New Directions for Community Colleges, no. 63.
Volume XVI, number 3.
San Francisco: Jossey-Bass, 1988.

New Directions for Community Colleges
Arthur M. Cohen, *Editor-in-Chief;* Florence B. Brawer, *Associate Editor*

New Directions for Community Colleges is published quarterly
by Jossey-Bass Inc., Publishers (publication number USPS 121-710),
in association with the ERIC Clearinghouse for Junior Colleges.
New Directions is numbered sequentially—please order extra copies
by sequential number. The volume and issue numbers above are
included for the convenience of libraries. Second-class postage paid
at San Francisco, California, and at additional mailing offices.
POSTMASTER: Send address changes to Jossey-Bass, Inc., Publishers,
350 Sansome Street, San Francisco, California 94104.

The material in this publication is based on work sponsored wholly
or in part by the Office of Educational Research and Improvement,
U.S. Department of Education, under contract number RI-88-062002.
Its contents do not necessarily reflect the views of the Department,
or any other agency of the U.S. Government.

Editorial correspondence should be sent to the Editor-in-Chief, Arthur
M. Cohen, at the ERIC Clearinghouse for Junior Colleges, University
of California, Los Angeles, California 90024.

Library of Congress Catalog Card Number LC 85-644753

International Standard Serial Number ISSN 0194-3081

International Standard Book Number ISBN 1-55542-882-7

Cover art by WILLI BAUM

Manufactured in the United States of America. Printed on acid-free paper.

Ordering Information

The paperback sourcebooks listed below are published quarterly and can be ordered either by subscription or single copy.

Subscriptions cost $60.00 per year for institutions, agencies, and libraries. Individuals can subscribe at the special rate of $45.00 per year *if payment is by personal check*. (Note that the full rate of $60.00 applies if payment is by institutional check, even if the subscription is designated for an individual.) Standing orders are accepted.

Single copies are available at $14.95 when payment accompanies order. (California, New Jersey, New York, and Washington, D.C., residents please include appropriate sales tax.) For billed orders, cost per copy is $14.95 plus postage and handling.

Substantial discounts are offered to organizations and individuals wishing to purchase bulk quantities of Jossey-Bass sourcebooks. Please inquire.

Please note that these prices are for the calendar year 1988 and are subject to change without notice. Also, some titles may be out of print and therefore not available for sale.

To ensure correct and prompt delivery, all orders must give either the *name of an individual* or an *official purchase order number*. Please submit your order as follows:

Subscriptions: specify series and year subscription is to begin.
Single Copies: specify sourcebook code (such as, CC1) and first two words of title.

Mail orders for United States and Possessions, Australia, New Zealand, Canada, Latin America, and Japan to:
Jossey-Bass Inc., Publishers
350 Sansome Street
San Francisco, California 94104

Mail orders for all other parts of the world to:
Jossey-Bass Limited
28 Banner Street
London EC1Y 8QE

New Directions for Community Colleges Series
Arthur M. Cohen, *Editor-in-Chief*
Florence B. Brawer, *Associate Editor*

CC1 *Toward a Professional Faculty,* Arthur M. Cohen
CC2 *Meeting the Financial Crisis,* John Lombardi
CC3 *Understanding Diverse Students,* Dorothy M. Knoell

CC4   *Updating Occupational Education,* Norman C. Harris
CC5   *Implementing Innovative Instruction,* Roger H. Garrison
CC6   *Coordinating State Systems,* Edmund J. Gleazer, Jr., Roger Yarrington
CC7   *From Class to Mass Learning,* William M. Birenbaum
CC8   *Humanizing Student Services,* Clyde E. Blocker
CC9   *Using Instructional Technology,* George H. Voegel
CC10 *Reforming College Governance,* Richard C. Richardson, Jr.
CC11 *Adjusting to Collective Bargaining,* Richard J. Ernst
CC12 *Merging the Humanities,* Leslie Koltai
CC13 *Changing Managerial Perspectives,* Barry Heermann
CC14 *Reaching Out Through Community Service,* Hope M. Holcomb
CC15 *Enhancing Trustee Effectiveness,* Victoria Dziuba, William Meardy
CC16 *Easing the Transition from Schooling to Work,* Harry F. Silberman, Mark B. Ginsburg
CC17 *Changing Instructional Strategies,* James O. Hammons
CC18 *Assessing Student Academic and Social Progress,* Leonard L. Baird
CC19 *Developing Staff Potential,* Terry O'Banion
CC20 *Improving Relations with the Public,* Louis W. Bender, Benjamin R. Wygal
CC21 *Implementing Community-Based Education,* Ervin L. Harlacher, James F. Gollatscheck
CC22 *Coping with Reduced Resources,* Richard L. Alfred
CC23 *Balancing State and Local Control,* Searle F. Charles
CC24 *Responding to New Missions,* Myron A. Marty
CC25 *Shaping the Curriculum,* Arthur M. Cohen
CC26 *Advancing International Education,* Maxwell C. King, Robert L. Breuder
CC27 *Serving New Populations,* Patricia Ann Walsh
CC28 *Managing in a New Era,* Robert E. Lahti
CC29 *Serving Lifelong Learners,* Barry Heermann, Cheryl Coppeck Enders, Elizabeth Wine
CC30 *Using Part-Time Faculty Effectively,* Michael H. Parsons
CC31 *Teaching the Sciences,* Florence B. Brawer
CC32 *Questioning the Community College Role,* George B. Vaughan
CC33 *Occupational Education Today,* Kathleen F. Arns
CC34 *Women in Community Colleges,* Judith S. Eaton
CC35 *Improving Decision Making,* Mantha Mehallis
CC36 *Marketing the Program,* William A. Keim, Marybelle C. Keim
CC37 *Organization Development: Change Strategies,* James Hammons
CC38 *Institutional Impacts on Campus, Community, and Business Constituencies,* Richard L. Alfred
CC39 *Improving Articulation and Transfer Relationships,* Frederick C. Kintzer
CC40 *General Education in Two-Year Colleges,* B. Lamar Johnson
CC41 *Evaluating Faculty and Staff,* Al Smith
CC42 *Advancing the Liberal Arts,* Stanley F. Turesky
CC43 *Counseling: A Crucial Function for the 1980s,* Alice S. Thurston, William A. Robbins
CC44 *Strategic Management in the Community College,* Gunder A. Myran
CC45 *Designing Programs for Community Groups,* S. V. Martorana, William E. Piland
CC46 *Emerging Roles for Community College Leaders,* Richard L. Alfred, Paul A. Elsner, R. Jan LeCroy, Nancy Armes
CC47 *Microcomputer Applications in Administration and Instruction,* Donald A. Dellow, Lawrence H. Poole

CC48 *Customized Job Training for Business and Industry,* Robert J. Kopecek, Robert G. Clarke
CC49 *Ensuring Effective Governance,* William L. Deegan, James F. Gollattscheck
CC50 *Strengthening Financial Management,* Dale F. Campbell
CC51 *Active Trusteeship for a Changing Era,* Gary Frank Petty
CC52 *Maintaining Institutional Integrity,* Donald E. Puyear, George B. Vaughan
CC53 *Controversies and Decision Making in Difficult Economic Times,* Billie Wright Dziech
CC54 *The Community College and Its Critics,* L. Stephen Zwerling
CC55 *Advances in Instructional Technology,* George H. Voegel
CC56 *Applying Institutional Research,* John Losak
CC57 *Teaching the Developmental Education Student,* Kenneth M. Ahrendt
CC58 *Developing Occupational Programs,* Charles R. Doty
CC59 *Issues in Student Assessment,* Dorothy Bray, Marcia J. Belcher
CC60 *Marketing Strategies for Changing Times,* Wellford W. Wilms, Richard W. Moore
CC61 *Enhancing Articulation and Transfer,* Carolyn Prager
CC62 *Issues in Personnel Management,* Richard I. Miller, Edward W. Holzapfel, Jr.

Contents

Editor's Notes 1
Janet E. Lieberman

Part 1. Framing the Issue

1. **Reconnecting Youth: The New Wave of Reform** 5
Frank Newman
A comprehensive review of the educational problems confronting the nation indicates the future role of higher education in making schools successful.

2. **History of the High School Connection** 13
Carol F. Stoel
The rich history of collaboration between secondary schools and colleges reveals some interesting trends and future concentrations.

3. **Opportunity for All** 25
James F. Gollattscheck
A national perspective emphasizing the numbers of students potentially in need demonstrates a new and significant role for the community college.

Part 2. Making Ordinary Students Winners

4. **Serving High-Risk Adolescents** 37
Cecilia Cullen, Martin G. Moed
Connectedness is the critical issue in servicing high-risk students in a collaboration. Restructuring the institutional framework to establish that connectedness demands conviction and creativity.

5. **Helping Students Learn** 51
Anne-Marie McCartan
Describing student involvement in new programs suggests more powerful learning strategies for high-risk students.

6. **Reaching Students: Communication from the Community Colleges** 61
Elizabeth A. Warren
A community college orientation program reaches out to secondary students in an effort to facilitate the transfer from high school to college.

7. **High School Students in College Courses: Three Programs** 69
Arthur Richard Greenberg
Research of some urban programs reveals the success and failures of three specific attempts to address the problems of the majority of students.

8. **New World School of the Arts: Beyond Dual Enrollment** 85
Katharine Muller
Special attention in an arts program highlights a new learning sequence for minority students.

9. **Enabling Professionalism: The Master Technician Program** 95
Doris K. Wimmer
Connections in technical programs provide an opportunity for increased professionalism among faculty.

10. **Merging Multiple Systems: Process and Problems** 101
Eunice B. Kirkbride
The problems uncovered in a cooperation between a multicampus college and a secondary school system suggest the need for careful attention to the process.

Index 113

Editor's Notes

In 1985 William T. Daly edited volume number 24 of New Directions for Teaching and Learning, *College-School Collaboration: Appraising the Major Approaches*. In the short interval of three years, a major surge of interest reflects concern in three areas: strong recommendations for closer connections by leading educators, heightened attention by college administrators, and a substantive increase in new joint programs. As the concept of collaboration expands, the collective experience broadens, and the opportunity to learn from concrete examples intensifies.

This volume presents a careful sampling of ideas and programs that provides background and realism to educators. Designed to encompass multiple perspectives and varied orientations, the chapters offer a broad survey of contemporary thinking and activity in the world of the high school-college connection.

An overview in the first section offers the theoretical and historical background of joint programs, documenting their importance on the national educational scene. Drawing from the philosophical foundations of American education, several national authorities emphasize the need for closer institutional ties to fulfill the promise of access and equity. The chronological reviews reveal the developmental growth of the concept of collaboration and anticipate some future trends.

In the second section, practitioners and researchers describe existing programs that highlight different perspectives. Concentrating on the practical how-to operation, college administrators demonstrate the steps in establishing collaborative programs. A broad spectrum of programs illustrates concentrations on technical and vocational sequences, orientations, student learning, arts, and improving professionalism. Other chapters of this section explain process, research, and assessment. (A sources and information chapter will not appear in this volume of *New Directions for Community Colleges* due to space constraints, but will resume as a regular feature in the Winter 1988 volume.)

Obviously, any one chapter represents only a segment of the total activity in the burgeoning field of high school-college connections. The U.S. Department of Education estimates 46,000 collaboratives nationwide. The contributors to this volume offer realistic yet idealistic observations of experienced and seasoned educators. In that spirit of pragmatic reform, the reader accesses recent learning about the high school-college connection.

Janet E. Lieberman
Editor

Janet E. Lieberman is the special assistant to the president for educational collaboratives at LaGuardia Community College.

Part 1.

Framing the Issue

A comprehensive review of educational problems confronting the nation indicates the future role of higher education in making schools successful.

Reconnecting Youth: The New Wave of Reform

Frank Newman

Perhaps the most intense period of educational reform ever seen in the United States has taken place over the past five or six years. Today, during what can be argued as the second wave of reforms, focus has shifted from the needs of typical students to the needs of minorities and at-risk students, to the issue of school restructuring, and to the quality of higher education, particularly undergraduate education. The LaGuardia Community College project involves all three aspects of reform.

While the attention span of Americans wanting reform efforts of any kind is typically short, throughout the country states seem committed to upgrading the educational system to meet needs imposed by the rapidly changing national demographics. In fact, the recent publication of reports by such groups as the Carnegie Forum and the National Governors Association suggest a continued sense of national urgency. Certainly, the sense of urgency is warranted.

When reform efforts began, we knew much less about what makes schools successful. A number of major research projects, such as Ted Sizer's (1985) work and John Goodlad's (1984) study of high schools, share a common thread—involvement: of the student in the active learning process, of teachers in the life of the school, of higher education professionals in successful programs, and of the business community in the dynamics of education.

The first wave of reform reflected a dual concern. First, the continual decline in test scores permeated education. Not only SAT scores, which garnered much of the attention, but test scores at every level had been declining for a decade and a half. The second concern was spawned by awareness that international competition would strain the United States' position of strength in the world market. In order to compete, the nation would have to concentrate on the quality of its education, which would play a critical role in the country's ability to remain a world leader.

One fascinating tendency of the United States is that it often has turned to education when facing a crisis. The Cold War was the first example of this tendency. Reacting to a perceived threat, Americans encouraged science and research in the universities, an emphasis supported by NASA chief scientist Wernher von Braun, who pointed out that our education system was failing us. This crisis reflected the powerful belief that education was the root cause of the nation's success, when the country was in trouble, better education could bail it out. Throughout the next domestic crisis, the struggle for civil rights, the United States looked again toward education for help. Today the onset of international competition continues this trend of focusing on education as a solution.

The emphasis in the first round of educational reform was on higher standards for students, so schools increased student testing. Since then, test scores have been increasing steadily with some very powerful and positive side effects. The recent National Assessment of Educational Progress studies, for example, show that in the past five years the amount of homework assigned to and done by students has approximately doubled. This is no mean feat; it is difficult to imagine how to increase the amount of homework done by students today without prompting intense debate about education. No state has passed laws requiring more homework, although several states have considered it.

The next focus of educational reform was on teachers themselves. Forty-two states now test teacher candidates before they can become certified. Many decisions, such as teacher certification, are made by states and are external to education institutions, yet they seriously affect the institutions.

Despite continuing criticism of the education system, America has responded again with more confidence in, and more money and prestige for, education. Three reasons can be cited for the turnaround. First, the demand for education is again escalating. Second, the educational reform process is not working for everyone. Third, educators understand from the lessons they have learned that much more work must be done to ensure successful education for everyone.

The second wave of reform, then, leads us to those students who were excluded from the first round of progress. Two distinct groups exist: minorities and at-risk youth. Although the tendency is to consider these groups identical, and, of course, an overlap exists, the two groups are not the same.

Statistically, schools do least well in educating blacks and Hispanics. Because these groups are the fastest-growing segment of the country's population, the future will be very difficult unless we address this problem. Small gains have been made in the past decade in the education of minorities, however. In elementary and secondary education, for example, the gap between black test scores and white test scores has been narrowing. The percentage of black students who graduate from high school has been increasing. Despite this progress, however, fewer black students are going on to college. Of those who go, fewer are graduating, and even fewer are entering or receiving degrees from graduate and professional schools. At the very time when the black population is increasing, our ability to serve this growing population is dangerously ineffective. Not only must minority access to education dramatically increase, but America must ensure that the people entering the professional and managerial life of this country are truly representative of the cultural diversity of the nation.

Even greater is the problem of at-risk students, those who are at risk of failing to make a successful transition to adulthood. The test for education is whether we create circumstances under which all students— or as close to all as possible—can become productive workers and citizens. This phenomenon is referred to as "disconnecting" in a report written by the Education Commission of the States (ECS). The report, *Reconnecting Youth: The Next Stage of Reform,* warns that students are not only failing to complete high school but are disconnecting from society (Business Advisory Commission, 1985). The tests used in defining failure and success are usually unemployment among youth and completion of high school. A long history of improvement of dropout rates prevails in this country, yet the problem is more critical than ever before.

For the more than 100 years since such statistics have been collected average dropout rates have decreased. The failure rate, once about 90 percent, fell gradually to around 40 percent by the end of World War II. This figure dropped to approximately 21 percent some fifteen years ago. Suddenly, however, dropout rates have swelled to some 28 percent of young adults. Why, at a time when more money than ever is spent on education should the rate of dropouts increase? At the heart of this problem are several familiar factors.

Although the United States has enjoyed a 24 percent increase in overall job production (as compared to 9 percent for Japan and virtually no growth for Western Europe), teenage unemployment is growing. We are magnets to the world; we draw people for jobs from every corner of the globe, yet we have rising teenage unemployment. This fact alone should trigger the notion that this is not simply structural unemployment.

When ECS began its at-risk project, it asked six economists to study the subject. These economists found a number of factors linked to teenage unemployment; the same was true with teenage arrests, suicides, and pregnancies. The facts were stark: Last year slightly more than 20 percent of live births were to unmarried young women ages twenty-two and younger—a devastating statistic.

Why do we have this problem? Teenage pregnancy and dropout rates are increasing fastest among whites and rapidly among Hispanics. Is it an urban problem? Actually, increasing teenage pregnancy and dropout rates are more serious problems on a percentage basis in some rural locations than they are in urban locations. Therefore these are not merely urban or suburban problems but world problems.

Determining what causes increased teenage pregnancy and dropout rates is a complex challenge with no one solution. One central argument revolves around the changing nature of the family structure. Consider a few worrisome facts: High-income married couples are most likely to nurture high-achieving children. The group next most likely to have high-achievers are parents whose resources are more limited. Less likely are single parents with resources and single parents without resources—the poor single-parent family, and the children least likely to succeed are those born to unmarried teenagers.

This spectrum includes the fact that the most affluent of these groups are waiting longer to have children. The median childbearing age has now increased to about twenty-six for the wealthiest category and that age is moving upward steadily. The median childbearing age for the poorest group has decreased from about age eighteen to as young as age sixteen and still decreasing. A second factor is that married couples are having fewer and fewer children: There are now two million more married couples without children than with children. Average-size families, by 1981 standards, now comprise just 4 percent of the current family units in the United States.

We are already experiencing major problems with dropouts and teenage pregnancy. Unless addressed, these problems will expand because children who fit our least-likely-to-succeed scenario will be entering the school system and accelerating the failure cycle. Altering that cycle is an urgent problem being considered by a growing body of researchers in the fields of sociology and psychology. One consideration about the failure cycle when this topic is raised in educational circles is that failure of the family is a societal problem. Should churches give thought to such problems? Should moral authorities in our country focus on these issues?

The problem of the failure cycle is actually the responsibility of the educational system. Looking at the size and scope of the problem, one can see that no other institution can better address the central part of the issue; no other institution has the track record of successful schools or is so intimately involved with students.

Clearly, schools have two obligations. One, they must take on the task of substituting, in a way, for the failures of the family. Two, they must take on the task of coordinating with social service agencies that deal with similar problems. Generally, educators do not like either of these options. They hold the traditional view that the families raise the children, love the children, encourage in them self-concepts of importance and success, and convince the children that school is important and can be mastered. Families feed and clothe children and get them to the bus stop. Schools have different responsibilities: accepting children, educating them during the day, keeping them safe, and returning them to their families. Our society is very uncomfortable crossing these conventional boundaries. Educators must, however, begin to make sure children feel loved, important, successful, and able to compete in the schooling process and in life, because there is no choice.

Common among at-risk students is the insecurity they feel about their future. At ECS we interviewed teenagers around the country, surveying their feelings about school. After reaching past the bravado, they expressed, with terrifying clarity, an enormous lack of self-esteem. Not only did they feel they were losers, but they felt they had no stake in the world. When one young man was asked why he was willing to support himself by crime, he said, "What difference does it make?" We asked, if nothing, wasn't he concerned that sooner or later he would end up in jail? He said candidly, "Yes, so what? I am probably not going to be around this world very long anyway?" When a young man in the prime of his life feels he is not going to be around very long, educators must take note. This leaves us with the question: Can schools be central in the process of helping students succeed? Obviously, the answer is yes, of course they can.

ECS is currently involved in a study that has found approximately 200 cases around the country where schools have been very successful at helping students succeed. One of the first examples was Middle College High School at LaGuardia Community College. But there are others of all sorts: effective pre-school programs, service corps programs, high schools, and junior high schools. A group of principals—each of whom had taken an existing high school, junior high school, or elementary school in terrible shape and made it a winner—recently met with a group of governors in Washington, D.C. We asked each to describe what the conditions had been like, how they began to change their schools, and what the results were. In every case the answer involved the formula described earlier: involvement of teachers in the life of the school, involvement of students in the life of the learning, and involvement at every level of the school. Most principals shared one unfortunate characteristic: They felt they had received very little support from the district and education system in general. Additional interviews with district officials confirmed this fact.

The principals succeeded despite the lack of support. They were charismatic individuals who pushed aside rules and worried more about students than reports. Involvement is central to going beyond the bureaucracy of the system to create circumstances under which success can occur.

Middle College students were interviewed and asked, "What is the difference here?" The answer was always, "This is the first place that ever took me seriously. This is the first place that ever told me that I was important to them. This is the first place where anybody ever expected anything of me."

When the educator is concerned with preparing students to be productive members of society, success involves much more than simply raising test scores. Students can pass limited test scores yet still be unable to function in society. Recent studies on reading skills and literacy report a 95 percent literacy rate in this country. The problem, however, is the level of literacy. Many people do not have higher-order literacy skills; that is, they do not possess the capacity to read, think, and use mathematics in ways that apply to daily life, particularly with daily life becoming more demanding.

What then is the role of higher education? Higher education administrators ought to be concerned about where students come from. If one considers the statistics, two factors are clearly apparent. First, the total number of eighteen-year-olds has peaked and is drifting downward. Second, the total number of at-risk students is drifting upward. Thus, there is a smaller body of people from which the country must draw its work force and college students of the future.

Although higher education has a major stake in determining the future, school reform must also involve elementary and secondary education. Each level is part of one education system. A benefit of the Ford Foundation's grant for Middle College, for example, is that it focuses on ways to make collaboration happen. Replicating this model and getting multiple parts of the system to work together is not an easy task.

We must be a country that faces change, boasts self-confidence, willingly takes risks, tries new ideas, and looks toward new directions. In order to educate people to meet those aims, we must address the problem in ways mentioned here, but also tackle the problem from a sociopolitical viewpoint. The world is much more complex than it used to be, and the complexity increases every day. Many problems like acid rain and toxic waste require a higher level of responsibility and involvement toward solutions. We simply must not tolerate having 20 percent of the population unable to understand and unwilling to be concerned with what is going on around them. A nation cannot function as a democracy if a significant part of its population is not involved in and feels no sense of responsibility to the society in which they live.

Although an antidote exists, the solutions will not come easily. Convinced that a problem is real, Americans look for solutions, reshape ideas, and find creative ways to make them work. The program at LaGuardia Community College is valuable in that it has found some answers. We need to learn what this institution has done, combine this information with ideas from other successful programs, and launch similar efforts across the country.

References

Business Advisory Commission. *Reconnecting Youth: The Next Stage of Reform.* Denver, Colo.: Education Commission of the States, 1985.

Goodlad, J. I. *A Place Called School: Prospects for the Future.* New York: McGraw-Hill, 1984.

Sizer, T. R. *Horace's Compromise, The Dilemma of the American High Schools.* Boston, Mass.: Houghton Mifflin, 1985.

Frank Newman is president of the Education Commission of the States, Denver, Colorado.

An observation of the evolution of high school–college connections, along with noteworthy examples, challenges the educator to consider the future direction of collaboration.

History of the High School Connection

Carol F. Stoel

On May 14 and 15, 1987 in a front page article of the *Washington Post*, Matthews covered the story of a successful high school–college connection: the Advanced Placement Exam. Begun in 1956 to serve elite students, these examinations have been recognized as a means for breaking the failure sequence that is familiar in urban and poor high schools across the country. In the barrage of reports and statistical analyses criticizing the future of our educational system, this story stands out for the promise it offers to the individual student and as the means it provides for tackling the systemic problems inherent in our educational system.

According to the *Washington Post*, a large number of students at Garfield High School in the barrio of Los Angeles, California, had again prepared for the Advanced Placement (AP) Exam. If history was an accurate predictor of the future, these students would "crush" the test. Recognizing the value of the AP Exam in raising expectations, a few teachers at Garfield had created an environment where success and accomplishment were the highest goals and where teacher and students could work together to gain victory over an outside opponent. Today 15 percent of the students at Garfield High take the examination, and a core of history, literature, language, mathematics, and science teachers challenges their Mexican-American students—whose parents probably never dreamed of going to college—to succeed on this examination.

The Advanced Placement Examinations are not new. In 1956, some 1,229 students from 1,104 high schools took 2,199 Advanced Placement Examinations. What is new is the growing number of students taking the exam, the expansion into a wide variety of fields, and the change of clientele from students of elite schools to students of all schools. According to the *Washington Post* in May 1987, some 250,000 students from 7,500 schools across the country took 350,000 exams. These schools represent one-third of all high schools in the country—a far cry from the elitist traditions of the program. While history and English remain the top choices of students taking the exam, calculus has moved into third place. The number of test-takers is still growing, a particularly encouraging sign given the sad state of mathematics education in this country. In a recent report by the National Research Council, chaired by Shirley A. Hill (1987, pp. 17-18), the following was stated: "The weak achievement test performance of our youngsters relative to those in other industrialized countries should jolt the American public. We hear that the average 12th grade mathematics student in Japan outperforms 95 percent of comparable U.S. 12th graders."

Preparation for these advanced classes must begin early if students are to have the time to master various sequences. The commitment from both the school and the students must begin in elementary school. According to the *Washington Post,* at Garfield High School the effects of the growing interest in the Advanced Placement Exams have been far-reaching. Teachers estimate that steadily rising test scores on standardized tests are due, in part, to the sense of rising expectations in the school and its community.

A quick review of the top high schools in the country that send students into the Advanced Placement Examination classroom shows the promise, but also the uniqueness, of a school like Garfield. A large percentage of Hispanic students take the exams at Garfield. Each time the challenge of teaching a new AP course is accepted, reverberations can be felt throughout the community and its schools.

For students, the implications of this high school–college connection are both substantive and emotional. The assurance of mastering a difficult, college-level examination can ease the transition to college enormously. In a survey conducted by Educational Testing Service (Willingham and Morris, 1986), transition to college was studied over a number of years, and the data indicated that those students who scored well on the AP Examinations performed better in college. Emotionally, this assurance is valuable for all students; however, for those first-time college students who worry whether they will be able to master the rigors of the college environment, this assurance is even more significant. Other programs that focus on the high school–college connection—LaGuardia Middle College is particularly noteworthy—aim to achieve the same sense of expectation and readiness. As Ernest Boyer (1983, p. 316) said in his high school study: "High schools do not carry on their work in isolation; they are connected to elementary and junior high schools and to higher education. In the end the quality of the American high school will be shaped in large measure by the qualities of these connections." Although we can understand what should go on between high school and college, we have lost sight of the true ramifications of this transition.

Past History

How to best prepare high school students for the institutions has always been a concern for educators. Historically, high schools developed on an ad hoc basis. In the West, where populations were scarce, it was literally impossible to pull together a large enough high school population to cover the material required to enter college. In California, the emphasis was on the lower school, and the secondary school was given short shrift. High schools were becoming more common in the East, but they still lacked focus and uniformity of curriculum. Additionally, because many higher education institutions were new and needed to bring in students, they were little more than secondary schools. In fact, preparatory programs were the rule of order on many campuses, some of which even gave college credit for the program—a situation we are familiar with today as we struggle with our remedial courses.

In many ways the situation today has not changed very much from those early days of high schools. The high school connection still is the focus for reconciling the divergent missions of two educational institutions, both struggling with new types of students, both needing to work together, but both also trying to maintain some level of autonomy.

As late as 1907, according to Brubacher and Willis (1968), over half the freshmen matriculated at Harvard, Yale, Princeton, and Columbia had failed to meet their entrance requirements in one field or another. Nevertheless, these prestigious institutions had found the same students desirable enough to bring to their campuses.

By 1870, some states, such as Michigan, tried to remedy the chaos that existed between high schools and colleges. Similar to the current work of some of our state legislatures today, Michigan sought to standardize college entrance requirements, which high schools had to satisfy if they wanted their graduates to be accepted by the University of Michigan. This state sought to make the secondary school the finishing ground for students preparing to go to college, an idea similar to the German model of the gymnasium. This attempt brought universities and high schools closer together, at least at the state level.

The New York State Regents Exams, begun in 1878, were another attempt to connect the programs of both high schools and colleges. Students could know ahead of time what the syllabus was and how to prepare for it. Requiring these exams was very successful in forcing certain issues to the fore, and created a sense of order in New York State, which is still associated with the Regents examination. By the 1880s, a number of states had developed organizations of colleges and secondary schools to examine questions of preparation and admissions standards. At that time, the Massachusetts Teachers Association passed two resolutions: One declared that the lack of cooperation between high schools and colleges was an "evil," and the second declared that increased cooperation between the schools and higher education would be a positive "good." As a result of these resolutions, the first high school-college meeting convened and established a national panel to bring together educators from both levels. This was the first of a number of meetings between 1893 and 1918 convened by the National Education Association (NEA). The Committee of Ten, as it was called, chaired by President Eliot of Harvard and made up of college leaders, examined the diversity and lack of commonality in secondary school curriculum and the state of articulation between secondary schools and colleges. The report in 1893 represented the first national attempt to standardize the high school curriculum and coordinate secondary and postsecondary education. Worrying that certain capable students might be discouraged from college, the report recommended that all subjects in the curriculum be taught in the same way and to the same extent. All subjects were to be taught in a manner to train the powers of observation, memory, expression, and reasoning.

Building on the emphases of the time, course completion and skill development, William Harper, president of the University of Chicago in 1892, restructured the university into a two-year junior and two-year senior college. Superior students could complete the junior program while they were in high school, and the average student could enter college after the eleventh grade. Twelve years after the initial move by the University of Chicago, only six high schools followed suit with articulation plans. A few colleges, however, were offering advanced placement.

In the 1900s, Nicholas Murray Butler, president of Columbia University, confessed that colleges could agree neither on "subjects to be offered for admission nor upon topics within these subjects" (Rudolph, 1968, p. 436). The situation for the preparatory schools at that time was equally sad. The principal of Phillips Academy of Andover complained bitterly about the diversity of college demands and the resulting prep school problems. All this agitation led to an 1899 meeting of the Association of Colleges and Secondary Schools of the Middle States and Maryland, where the College Entrance Examination Board was created. Its function was to establish a series of tests that all colleges could use to determine the preparedness of students for admission to their institutions. High school representatives sat on all committees for preparing subject examinations. The acceptance of tests used by all colleges was slow in coming, and for many years individual colleges continued to use their own tests to determine a student's preparedness. But over time, the fact that students could take the tests in a variety of geographic locations for applications for admission to any college became a significant source of support for the tests. Thus, college interests continued to dominate high schools even though most high school students never dreamed of attending college.

Even as the college preparatory mission appeared to be growing in strength in the late nineteenth century, confusion and mixed messages about the proper role of the high school continued to abound. While major forces attempted to determine expectations for the high school, the growing movement toward universal education pervaded the atmosphere. In a report by another committee of the NEA in 1911, the issue of the dual responsibilities of the high schools was raised again. The committee reported that "the dominating position of colleges still laid too heavy a burden on the secondary school in asking it to prepare all students for life at the same time it was preparing some for college." Consequently, the committee demanded an open-door policy so that "the secondary school might have as much freedom to explore the adolescent's possibilities for self-realization as the college claimed for itself" (Brubacher and Willis, 1968, p. 252). Nevertheless, it was not until 1918 that this perspective became more of a reality.

With the report of the National Education Association's Commission for the Reorganization of Secondary Education, the committee—now dominated by public school leaders—made clear its position on expanding access to higher education. They saw "democracy demanding that liberal education be extended to an increasingly large segment of the population" (Brubacher and Willis, 1968, p. 253). The committee predicted that higher education would need to take on an increasing number of students just as secondary education had over the last fifty years.

The spirit of populism and optimism that has driven so much of the development of American education was alive, but it did not resolve the thorny issues. High schools and colleges were confounded by mixed purposes and by conflicting popularities, all with differing expectations. Throughout the Depression years, World War II, and the great GI Bill, the sorting between college and high school continued. Too many GIs, who flunked their first year of classes understood this sorting. It foretold the revolving door drama of the 1960s and 1970s, when high schools and colleges could not meet the needs of students. At each step confusion remained, and the door was more easily opened than passed through to the other side.

Modern History

The Sputnik crisis brought a brief interlude of common sense and the first major governmental programs aimed at creative cooperation between high schools and colleges. With generous federal funding, high school teacher institutes were established at colleges and universities. Science and language programs dominated the field and were funded by the National Defense Education Act. As is true today, the fear of competition from other nations overshadowed the educational agenda and forced action. Although many teachers enjoyed the opportunities to study and collaborate with others in their field, the education crisis abated with our successful ventures on the moon. The cooperative programs were curtailed and finally dropped and teaching itself became a most unpopular endeavor.

The mid sixties proved to be a fertile time for innovations that sought to focus on individual growth and learning needs of students through the high school–college connection. Simon's Rock Early College was founded in 1964 by Elizabeth B. Hall because she recognized the need for more educational options for adolescents and strongly believed in the college's responsibility to promote emotional, as well as intellectual, growth. Students interested in early college admission found an appropriate college suited to their needs.

Upward Bound, first funded by foundations and later by the U.S. government, took its roots from the same belief that expanding higher education opportunities was important and that colleges should offer an intellectual and emotional support structure to assist students who would not otherwise be admitted to college. In this case, high school students spent summers on campuses to prepare for college admission. Over the last fifteen years, federal support for the program has been maintained; however, the level of funding has remained too low for the program to influence the necessary systemic changes and reach the appropriate number of students.

Nevertheless, personnel from these and similar programs maintained the high school–college connection for such first-time college students and less aggressive high school students. These individuals conducted the writing, remedial math, counseling, and special programs designed to ease the transition from high school to college, but for the most part worked within the more traditional academic structure.

The impetus for the major innovative programs of the 1970s grew from a deep sense of the limitations and rigidity of the larger system. Although programs like Upward Bound were making progress, the number of students reached remained very small, the cost seemed high, and the dropout situation worsened. Programs like Middle College at LaGuardia Community College were aimed at serving a different kind of learner. Data from a research report funded by the Ford Foundation indicates that over the past ten years Middle College at LaGuardia has been successful. In a sample of 176 Middle College graduates, 75 percent have either completed their associate degree or have had some participation in higher education (Clark, 1988). Other colleges and cities around the country are seeking to replicate this model. The strong focus on student expectations and providing assistance to meet challenges have been the hallmarks of the program. Students who were on the verge of dropping out have discovered in the atmosphere of a small, positive school a new strength within themselves. The focus, similar to that of the Advanced Placement Exam, is on student gains. The programs at Middle College are learner-centered and produce results.

Other successful programs of the 1980s have paid more attention to teachers and administrators, hoping to develop their perspective about the relevance of the high school–college connection and provide opportunities for shared learning experiences. The National Association for State Universities and Land Grant Colleges has worked with fourteen communities to help chief executive officers of both college and high school systems influence and support collaboration. At the Yale New Haven Institute, school faculty spend time at Yale developing curricular expertise in a topic of their choice. In the last ten years, the National Endowment for the Humanities has funded a series of summer institutes in which high school teachers gather with college faculty on campuses for in-depth study of various disciplines.

Trends and Future Directions

In the last few years, education has received an unprecedented amount of attention in the media and politics. Educators must focus on significant points of transition where results can be measured and futures estimated. The high school–college transition offers one of the most revealing moments for this analysis, and results of current data are not positive. Most devastating to the past fifteen years of work is a recent study by the American Council on Education (Wilson, 1987), reporting that the percentage of eighteen- to twenty-four-year-old black high school graduates entering college in 1985 decreased to 26 percent from 34 percent in 1976. During a ten-year period, the proportion of blacks in this age group graduating from high school increased from about 68 percent to 75.6 percent. Similar trends existed among Hispanics, the study maintains. At the same time more Hispanics were graduating from high school, the proportion entering college decreased from 36 percent in 1976 to 27 percent in 1985. The future must yield improvements if the nation is to meet the challenges of the twenty-first century.

As we look at future trends in the high school–college connection, one must bear in mind we are not talking about only the smartest students or the near dropouts. This connection is important for all students because at this juncture we see great opportunity in the summation of one phase and the attempt to interlock with a new structure. In establishing new goals for the educational system, we must also consider that the end result is improving the quality of education for all students and that the difficult questions of academic emphasis and resource allocation cannot be overlooked merely to simplify decisions. As legislators and high-level politicians become more involved, a balance must be struck between the needs of individual students and of the larger system. The firm demands of politicians for accountability and quality are a breath of fresh air in a troubled system.

Conversations about the high school-college connection have never been more substantive nor more inspired. From Carnegie's high school study (Boyer, 1983) to California State School Superintendent Honig's war on textbook manufacturers, we are seeing a serious appraisal of what should be the content of the various courses students are taking. Criticism abounds on the quality of present textbooks; the major complaint is that textbooks are overloaded with facts without much thought given to developing principles or theory. The response, of course, has been that this emphasis on facts is what is required in college. Unfortunately, the overabundance of information continues in colleges, without considering how students will use all this information once they are in the workplace, laboratory, or office. And in spite of all the emphasis on facts, recent books have decried the fact that our youth share so little of a common culture and knowledge.

Major study groups, such as at the National Academy of Science, are attempting to look at these issues and draw some conclusions shortly about the math curriculum. Goaded by the fear that Americans are rapidly falling behind the Japanese, industrial and educational leaders are pressing for a sequenced educational program that allows our students to excel and to keep up with the state of the art.

Changing demographics are and will continue to be a major factor in influencing the future of education. The overall shrinking number of young people, the growing number of minority and white students from poor and undereducated backgrounds, and the declining number of white middle-class children forms a backdrop against which all future educational and political decisions need to be made. With the aging American population, the concern for who will continue to "run the store" will influence many important decisions about educational reform and funding.

Legislatures have entered into this conversation as well. As they struggle to find solutions to the economic development questions of their states, they are looking at the high school-college connection as an indicator of how successful their state has been in producing a climate that has promise for the future. Looking for indicators of success, they are examining tests and standard objectives that they can impose on both the K-12 system and the collegiate system. They believe it is often easier for legislators to see the relationship between the two systems than for administrators. Their influence in allocating funds will increase with the ability to evaluate success by outcomes of student test scores, by the number of students in growing and high-demand areas such as math and science, and by dropout and graduation rates. Types and amounts of financial aid will become a major issue over the next years as Congress attempts to cut back the deficit and states require educated personnel to create opportunities for economic advancement.

With growing cynicism about the quality of higher education, legislators are not reluctant to ask colleges and universities to comply with certain expectations. Basic skills and remedial courses are far less acceptable to legislators today than they were years ago, and we are seeing a clear delineation of what is appropriate for high school and for college. Unfortunately, it is no more possible today than in earlier times for high schools to meet all the basic skill needs of their students. The combination of developmental needs, timing, educational problems, and other factors make it extremely difficult to delineate between the two sectors as clearly as some critics would like. In fact, those programs like Middle College, which provide a transitional bridge, are the most likely to make it possible for weaker or underprepared students to make the transition. Middle College is becoming a popular option in which various states can invest. Having been tested for over fifteen years, the college offers a proven example of how to keep students in school; in fact, Middle College provides an opportunity for all students to excel. As more legislators see that the funding is within their limits if the same educational dollars are simply being used in a more flexible manner, the model will continue to be adopted and modified. A student-oriented program like Middle College will influence other facets of the system as well; educators who recognize that higher academic expectations can lead to success will follow the lead.

The Advanced Placement Examinations offer the promise of high expectations, hard work, and results. The positive effects of the examination process on individual students and teachers at Garfield High School can be expected at other schools as well. In this time of insecurity about the educational system, testing seems to be the one thing that people are ready to support. The AP tests have won the confidence of both the high school and the college community by being reliable measures of what has been learned. We can expect their use to continue to grow, as will any other form of testing that conveys the same reliability.

The teacher will continue to be the focus of the studies and critiques on the state of education. The role of the college in preparing the K-12 teacher will continue to dominate the discussion as means are sought to improve the quality of teaching as well as the content of what is taught. Interesting, albeit limited, examples of creative and successful collaborations between faculty and teachers exist today (for example, the Yale New Haven project and the National Endowment for the Humanities secondary-school teachers program). The collaborative nature of these programs, emphasizing content and professionalism, promises innovations in the overall atmosphere of schools. Whether they can be expanded to be a routine part of a teacher's existence remains to be seen. The National Science Foundation programs of the earlier years failed to sustain themselves. Perhaps we have learned an important lesson and these new programs will reach out to more teachers every year. Certainly the crisis in teaching, which tells us that we are no longer getting or able to retain truly qualified personnel, suggests that support programs are badly needed. These support programs may not only help retain good teachers, but in some cases may actually transmit content that is essential for teachers to do the job.

The connection between high school and college could not be more important than it is today. Leaders of higher education institutions realize this. In September, 1987, at the Spring Hill Gathering, thirty-seven college presidents joined together to make a statement about the significance of teaching to the future of America and to commit themselves and their institutions to active roles. This is a major new step and one that augurs well. Through their research capacities, the examples their faculty set in teaching undergraduates, and ongoing, long-term relationships, they can make a big difference.

Funds are necessary to carry out many of the new initiatives that are developing and that show promise. In Congress an understanding and willingness to look at some of these needs exists and private funding sources, such as the Rockefeller Foundation, are making teaching a high priority. The sense of urgency that surrounds education today is promising, as long as it does not burn itself out. We are facing serious issues that deserve serious attention.

References

Boyer, E. *High School: A Report on Secondary Education in America.* New York: Harper & Row, 1983.

Brubacher, J. S., and Willis, R. *Higher Education in Transition.* New York: Harper & Row, 1968.

Clark, T. A. "The Influence of Middle College High School on the Work and Postsecondary Experiences of Graduating Classes from 1977 to 1986." LaGuardia Community College, Long Island City, N.Y., 1988.

Hill, S. A. *Newsreport.* Washington, D.C.: National Research Council, 1987, *37* (6), 17-18.

Matthews, J. "Tests Help Ordinary School Leap Ahead." *Washington Post,* May 14, 1987.

Matthews, J. "A Teacher Using Challenge of Calculus Alters Equation of Inner-City Learning." *Washington Post,* May 15, 1987.

Rudolph, F. *The American College and University.* New York: Knopf, 1968.

Willingham, W., and Morris, M. *College Board Report Four Years Later: A Longitudinal Study of Advanced Placement Students in College.* Princeton, N.J.: College Entrance Exam Board, 1986.

Wilson, R. *Sixth Annual Status Report on Minorities in Higher Education.* Washington, D.C.: American Council on Education, 1987.

Carol F. Stoel is director of the American Association of University Women Educational Foundation. Previously, she worked at the University of Maryland, Hood College, and with the Fund for the Improvement of Postsecondary Education.

A national perspective emphasizing the numbers of students potentially in need demonstrates a new and significant role for the community college.

Opportunity for All

James F. Gollattscheck

Promise of Opportunity for All

Opportunity for all is a concept that has existed in the minds of certain men and women for most of recorded history. One can find examples in the Bible and in the thought and writings of Greek philosophers from before the birth of Christ. Plato and Socrates stress the dignity and worth of the human spirit. The events that led to the signing of the Magna Carta in England in 1215 and the French Revolution at the end of the eighteenth century also set the stage for the rebellion of the English colonies in America and the creation of the first nation to be established on the stated premise that men are equal and deserving of equal opportunity. Earlier struggles for equal opportunity usually involved opposition to governmental authority. With the establishment of the United States of America, even that authority was to be in the hands of the people.

From the beginning, American leaders placed their faith in education, not only as a premise upon which the concept of self-government rests, but as the guarantor of continued progress toward a full concept of opportunity. Indeed, the history of education in the United States is as true and accurate a reflection of the development of the concept of opportunity for all in our nation as one can find. The Constitution of the United States is silent on the issue of education, regarding it as the responsibility of individual states, an assumption based more on a strong concern for protecting individual rights than on a lack of concern for education. Education was one of those powers that was, by virtue of the tenth amendment to the Constitution, explicitly "reserved to the States" (Hoffman, 1987, p. 447).

At any time in its history, the nature and extent of a nation's commitment to education and to equal opportunity may be characterized rather easily by its answers to two simple questions: Who should be taught and what should they be taught? More specifically, who should be provided with what educational opportunities at public expense?

In the eighteenth century and for most of the nineteenth, not even the most farsighted and liberal-minded visionaries could foresee that the general citizenry would ever need more than a grade school education. Higher education was for the select few and concentrated on religion, philosophy, and literature. Harvard University, founded by colonists "dreading to leave an illiterate Ministry to the Churches, when our present Ministers shall lie in the Dust" (*New England's First Fruits*, 1643), served as a model for all of American higher education. In 1862 the Morrill Act, known widely as the Land-Grant Colleges Act, broke the monopoly of classical traditions in higher education by calling for the establishment of higher education institutions dedicated to instruction in agriculture and the mechanic arts in each state. For the first time, the "what" of American higher education had been changed.

The question of "who" should be educated was also changing, but more slowly. By the end of the first half of the twentieth century the belief that every American citizen should have the opportunity for a free public school education through high school was almost universal. That this concept was not always well implemented was not a real concern to most Americans. What was important and new in the history of education was that the opportunity was there. In the 1940s and 1950s two things happened that radically changed America's view of who should have access to higher education—the Servicemen's Readjustment Act of 1944, popularly known as the GI Bill, and the development of comprehensive community colleges.

The GI Bill made a college education possible for a larger mass of citizens than ever before, and never again would it be possible for higher education in America to be considered solely the preserve of the privileged. But the GI Bill was a student-financial aid measure and not an educational movement. It brought about no changes in education other than those caused by the sheer numbers of students descending on the nation's colleges and universities. The development of the comprehensive community college, however, has had a twofold impact: It has brought postsecondary education within financial and geographic reach of a larger number of students, and it has brought about important educational changes. The open-door policy of most community colleges, combined with an emphasis on occupational programs and community services, has added a new dimension to American higher education (Gollattscheck, Harlacher, Roberts, and Wygal, 1976).

It is strange that, in a nation whose constitution reserves matters of education to its states, several of America's major developments in education—the Northwest Ordinance, the Morrill Act, and the GI Bill—have been results of federal legislation. The community college movement also was spurred on at the national level, but this time by executive action rather than by legislation. The President's Commission on Higher Education, appointed by President Truman in 1946, called for "the opening of doors of higher education to members of society who, throughout American history, had lingered on the periphery of the American dream of equality for all; members of lower socioeconomic groups, blacks, women, working adults, and other segments of society would have educational opportunities previously denied them if the commission's goals were adopted. A number of the goals would be achieved through an expanded network of two-year colleges. These colleges were to be so closely tied and committed to serving their communities that the Commission labeled them *community colleges*" (Vaughan, 1983, p. 21).

The civil rights movement of the 1950s and 1960s was played out in America's schools and colleges, and many of the landmark victories involved education. A historic and unanimous decision of the United States Supreme Court in 1954 ruled that racial segregation in public schools was unconstitutional as a violation of the Fourteenth Amendment clause guaranteeing equal protection of the laws. In 1962 the admission of James Meredith as the first black student at the University of Mississippi required the presence of 3,000 federal troops, but overt racial discrimination in public higher education was ended. The battle to overcome de facto segregation continues today and is one of the themes of this volume.

Failure of the Promise

The preceding paragraphs have outlined very sketchily the efforts of a nation to make and keep a promise, through education, that all its citizens would have an equal opportunity for what the nation's founders called "happiness," but in today's language would probably be called "quality of life." Has the promise been kept? The answer is yes and no. More citizens of this nation have greater opportunities than at any time in the history of any nation and certainly more than its founders could possibly have imagined. That this volume has been written, however, is a clear indication that many people today, particularly educators, are still unsatisfied with the keeping of the promise.

The difference between a record of unparalleled opportunity and our lack of satisfaction with that record seems to be that of an expanded understanding and expectation of what is meant by opportunity. It is true that no American is ostensibly excluded from educational opportunities all the way through to a college education. Public school education is available to all and legally required up to a specified age in every state. Community, technical, and junior colleges with their open admissions have made a college education a possibility for almost every citizen. Yet there are clear indications that barriers exist that prevent many people from taking advantage of these opportunities. We realize that race, socioeconomic status, level of education of one's parents, where one lives, the quality of one's early education, and many other factors combine to determine the likelihood of one's being able to take advantage of existing educational opportunities. Our present concept of opportunity for all requires us now to seek out and attempt to remove those barriers.

Among the clearest indicators and most pervasive arguments that all citizens do not have equal opportunity are the number of young people who do not complete high school, the number of those who do but are not academically capable of going further in education or finding adequate employment, and the magnitude of the adult illiterate population in America.

Current educational literature is filled with reports and recommendations about high school dropouts. One recent report, *What to Do About Youth Dropouts?*, was published by the Structured Employment/Economic Development Corporation and distributed by the Hispanic Policy Development Project. It is a summary extracted from *Keeping Students in School*, by Margaret Terry Orr. In the report, Orr (1987, p. 7) emphasizes that, "dropouts are not a small problem segment of our country's adolescents." Of all students entering high school, 14 to 25 percent will not complete. Of the 3.3 million students graduating from the ninth grade in 1983, some 470,000 to 830,000 will drop out. In 1983 there were 16.8 million youth aged eighteen to twenty-one. Of this group, as many as 4 million had been or were still high school dropouts.

Of critical importance to those concerned with equality of opportunity is an examination of who drops out of school. Orr (1987, p. 7) tells us:

> Obviously, some students are more likely to drop out than are others. According to the High School and Beyond Survey, a national longitudinal survey of 30,000 randomly selected 1980 sophomores: Fourteen percent of sophomores will drop out, including 12 percent of whites, 17 percent of blacks, and 19 percent of Hispanics. Urban youth are 50 percent more likely to drop out than are rural youths. White students in the South and West are almost 40 percent more likely to drop out than are those in the

Northeast and the North Central states, while the reverse is true for black students. Youth who are least prepared economically and educationally are most likely to drop out. For example, 22 percent of students from low-income families will drop out, in contrast to only 7 percent of those from upper-income families. Students who drop out are about twice as likely as those who do not to have a parent who never completed high school. Students who score low on achievement tests are six times as likely to drop out as those who score higher.

From these few but compelling facts, clearly a minority student entering junior high school, who lives in and attends school in an inner city, who comes from a low-income family, whose parents did not go far in school, and whose academic achievement level is low—the majority of junior high school students in America's large urban centers—has far from an equal likelihood of completing high school as his or her white, suburban counterpart. A poor white student in the rural South might not fare much better.

The same factors that influence the probability of dropping out cause some students who do graduate to leave school with serious deficiencies in academic skills. A recent item in *USA Today* was headlined " 'Defect Rate' 50% from USA Schools" and reported on a speech by Xerox chairman David Kearns, in which he described schools as "a failed monopoly," producing workers "with a 50 percent defect rate" (Ordovensky, 1987, p. 1A).

Whether we agree with Kearns or not, the fact is he represents an opinion held by many in industry and in the general public. The percentage of high school graduates entering community, technical, and junior colleges needing developmental education lends credence to the criticism. These high school graduates, who lack the academic skills usually associated with high school graduation, will not have much more opportunity for success than their colleagues who dropped out.

Another key indicator of our failure to deliver on the promise of opportunity for all is the number of adult illiterates in America. In the materials developed for a recent national video teleconference ("American Association . . . ," 1987, p. 6A), the American Association of Community and Junior Colleges (AACJC) emphasized the following points:

- The United States has the highest illiteracy rate among industrialized nations
- Thirteen percent of America's work force is illiterate
- The United States has an estimated 23 million adults who cannot read beyond the fourth grade level and another 45 million who cannot read beyond the eight grade level
- Some 400,000 new individuals move into the adult illiterate group each year.

The adult illiterate is part of the group we now call the at-risk population. By *at risk* we mean those people who for whatever reason already are, or are likely to become, incapable of self-support and of participating as effective citizens in our democratic society. We find these at-risk citizens among high school dropouts, illiterates, immigrants and refugees, displaced homemakers, single parents, people with disabilities, the elderly, and other minority groups. Those in the at-risk population clearly do not have an equal opportunity.

In the Harry S. Truman Lecture celebrating the first National Community College Month, Arthur Flemming, former secretary of the Department of Health, Education, and Welfare, singled out one group—the at-risk youth—when he said, "The seriousness of teenage unemployment is clear to all of us. The teenage unemployed are a major component of the underclass, *the magnitude of which constitutes a major threat to the political, economic, social, and moral underpinnings on which our nation rests"* (1986, p. 8).

Renewing the Promise

At the same time that our concept of what constitutes opportunity for all is expanding, we are beginning to understand that the loss of opportunity affects not only the individual but society as well. When we help an individual gain an education, find adequate employment, and become a productive, participating citizen, we remove a liability from our society and replace it with an asset. A telling point made in the AACJC video teleconference on adult illiteracy ("American Association . . . ," 1987, p. 6A) was that adult illiteracy costs our nation an estimated $225 billion a year in lost industrial productivity, unrealized tax revenues, welfare, crime, poverty, and related social ills.

In a 1985 publication of the Business Advisory Commission of the Education Commission of the States (1985, p. 8) entitled *Reconnecting Youth: The Next Stage of Reform,* it was suggested that our nation faces a declining youth population with an increasing at-risk segment, while at the same time a rising business demand exists for entry-level employees.

> The problem, simply stated is this: A growing proportion of our young people are not making successful transitions to productive adult lives. They are paying a heavy price. We, as a society, are paying a heavy price. In the years ahead, the costs are going to get higher.
>
> In 1978 young adults constituted 23 percent of the U.S. population. By 1995 they will constitute only 16 percent, shrinking by one-quarter the size of the entry-level labor pool. Within that shrinking labor pool is a growing pool of at-risk young men and women: people in their teens and early twenties who could become productive citizens but most likely will not unless something out of the ordinary happens. They have the intelli-

gence to succeed, but they lack important skills, family support, discipline, and the motivation to make it. An unconscionably disproportionate number of them are poor, black, and Hispanic youth.

A recent publication, funded by the U.S. Department of Labor, makes the same point forcefully with the following contrasting predictions for the twenty-first century.
- The work force will grow slowly, becoming older, more female, and more disadvantaged. Only 15 percent of the new entrants to the labor force over the next thirteen years will be native white males, compared to 47 percent in that category today.
- The new jobs in service industries will demand much higher level skills than the jobs of today. Very few new jobs will be created for those who cannot read, follow directions, and use mathematics. Ironically, the demographic trends in the work force, coupled with the higher-skill requirements of the economy, will lead to both higher and lower unemployment: more joblessness among the least skilled and less among the most educationally advantaged (Johnston and Packer, 1987, p. xiii).

Educators long concerned with the needs and problems of individuals are now finding allies in businessmen and politicians concerned with profits and losses and with economic development. Thus there is a new coalition committed to seeing that all Americans do indeed have an equal opportunity.

What Can the New Coalition Do? The Business Advisory Commission of the Education Commission of the States (1985, pp. 5-6) challenged educators, business leaders, and policymakers to:

> raise the visibility of this problem, sponsor debate, replicate successful programs, and take the necessary risks to get people moving. . . . Leaders in education are called upon to 'get it right the first time,' [and] head off disconnection with effective early education, alternative schools, and dropout programs. Schools are challenged to move reform into a new phase that connects at-risk students more directly with adults and the larger worlds of work and culture. Business and labor leaders are challenged to make the first work experiences of youth positive experiences, to steer dropouts back into school and to enter into training networks. Business and labor leaders have much to share with schools in need of restructuring. They are encouraged to offer their expertise in management, reorganization, decentralization, financing of innovations, personnel evaluation, and labor negotiations in the interest of change. Policymakers are challenged to enable all of the foregoing initiatives to take place. Policy in diverse areas must be examined for its influence on youth, streamlined and strengthened to address more effectively the problem of at-risk youth.

Because educators are most likely to be involved with youth at all stages of their development and because it is the business of educators to be concerned with the youth of the nation, educators not only should but must take the lead in forming and guiding the coalition to address the problem of at-risk youth. Clearly, considering the magnitude and complexity of the problem, education alone cannot provide effective and long-lasting solutions to the problem. It is equally obvious that within education no one sector can address the problem effectively in isolation. Only through the concerted efforts of all educational sectors working together in partnerships with business, labor, and policymakers will the conditions that cause youth to become at risk be examined and changed. The danger to the economy, security, and well-being of this nation is so clear and present that it is time to lay aside the so-called terrible T's— trust, tradition, and turf—which have so often precluded cooperative endeavors in the past, and begin to work together to find ways to prevent the disconnection of some youth and to reconnect those already at risk.

What Can Community, Technical, and Junior Colleges Do? These colleges are in a unique and key position to provide leadership to the coalition. They work closely with both secondary schools and universities; they work with community organizations and institutions; they have established partnerships with business, industry, and labor; they have developed programs to rescue the academically deficient; and they serve youth and adults of all ages; they already serve a sizeable population of at-risk students. Most important, community, technical, and junior colleges have the commitment.

References

"American Association of Community and Junior Colleges Advertisement." *USA Today*, June 19, 1987, p. 6A.

Business Advisory Commission. *Reconnecting Youth: The Next Stage of Reform.* Denver, Colo.: Education Commission of the States, 1985.

Flemming, A. S. *Community Colleges: The Untold American Story.* Washington, D.C.: American Association of Community and Junior Colleges, 1986.

Gollattscheck, J. E., Harlacher, E. L., Roberts, E., and Wygal, B. R. *College Leadership for Community Renewal: Beyond Community-Based Education.* San Francisco: Jossey-Bass, 1976.

Hoffman, M. S. (ed.). *World Almanac and Book of Facts.* New York: Pharos Books, 1987.

New England's First Fruits. London: Printed by R. O. and G. D. for H. Overton, 1643.

Ordovensky, P. " 'Defect Rate' 50% from USA Schools." *USA Today*, Oct. 27, 1987, p. 1A.

Orr, M. T. (ed.). *Keeping Students in School: A Guide to Effective Dropout Prevention Programs and Services.* San Francisco: Jossey-Bass, 1987.

Vaughan, G. B. "Historical Perspective: President Truman Endorsed Community College Manifesto." *Community and Junior College Journal*, 1983, 53 (7), 21-24.

James F. Gollattscheck is executive vice-president and association treasurer of the American Association of Community and Junior Colleges.

Part 2.

*Making Ordinary
Students Winners*

Connectedness is the critical issue in servicing high-risk students in a collaboration. Restructuring the institutional framework to establish that connectedness demands conviction and creativity.

Serving High-Risk Adolescents

Cecilia Cullen, Martin G. Moed

Overview

A great deal of publicity has been given to New York City's high school dropout problem. The attrition statistics vary from 39 percent to 60 percent and become even more pronounced, sometimes reaching 90 percent, at schools that are unselective and generally serve the poor. This dilemma exists in varying degrees in all of the country's larger and older cities, and everyone agrees that finding approaches to keep urban young people in high school is a major objective that must be met. At the same time, recent studies describe high schools as being the same as they were a century ago. Students sit in rows, listen to teachers, and copy information into notebooks. This information is then committed to memory, and students are evaluated with tests. While it is generally understood that students learn by doing, schools continue to give only vicarious experience in the form of summarization of primary sources, science demonstrations, films, filmstrips, and slides.

In order to reach this group of disenfranchised students, Middle College High School has combined the resources of a high school and a college to reconnect youth. While still in high school, students are connected to their future by attending college classes on a college campus which improves self-image, makes college a realistic goal, and provides motivation to finish high school. Through a career education program, students are connected to the working world, enabling the school to use the student's work experiences to improve their attitudes and skills. The program develops a sense of responsibility and promotes the ethic of student-as-worker. A counseling program provides interaction among peers and the adults in the school community so that the student becomes engaged in his or her own education. The results of this unique program have been dramatic. Attendance is high, the dropout rate is low (less than 7 percent), and transition to college is high (about 80 percent).

Middle College High School began in 1974, testing the hypothesis that a supportive collaborative relationship between a college and a high school could reduce the attrition rate of students considered to be potential dropouts. It opened after two years of planning by Janet Lieberman and other educators and was funded by the Carnegie Corporation and the Fund for the Improvement of Postsecondary Education. At first, Middle College High School resembled a small, traditional high school. As the school evolved, it developed its own identity. The college assumed the role of a caring parent, careful not to impose itself on the maturing child, but ever ready with advice, direction, assistance, and resources when needed. Because of this solicitous relationship, the school has identified its own mission and has experimented and developed beyond the scope of a traditional high school.

Middle College serves 450 students and is funded and staffed using the same formula as other alternative high schools operated by the Board of Education of the City of New York. Use of similar funding as other units was important to prove that the school could be replicated without additional financing. Faculty and staff are paid by the board of education, with the principal, teachers, and administrators hired from the pool of eligible high school personnel. Administrative costs—such as heat, light, phones, supplies, furniture, and postage—are paid by the college.

Middle College is housed in one of the three buildings that compose LaGuardia Community College of the City University of New York. The main campus of Middle College is located in New York City's borough of Queens. The high school occupies approximately 20,000 square feet, and its facilities include one administrative office and nineteen classrooms spread over two floors. Middle College students have free access to all parts of the LaGuardia campus, and college students take classes in the Middle College areas as well. The layout gives students a home base, but does not impose strict boundaries.

Middle College has all the benefits of being a small operating unit without experiencing any of the disadvantages because it draws on the resources of a larger institution. Middle College students are fully participating members of the community college with all the privileges and responsibilities. They are given college IDs and have access to all college facilities—library, science and computer laboratories, cafeterias, recreational facilities, a theater, language laboratories, and newspaper layout facilities. These resources are normally unavailable to inner-city high school students.

Another major advantage of a high school located on a college campus is the improvement in discipline. Initially, tenth graders have trouble adjusting to freedom of movement and lack of control. At Middle College, no one is prohibited from walking the halls during classes or from smoking, and there are no bells between classes. Experience has shown that within a short time Middle College students adopt the behavior of the larger student body. Except for the occasional adolescent incident, the behavior of the high school student closely resembles that of college students enrolled at LaGuardia Community College.

To facilitate individual attention and cope with significant skill deficits, Middle College classes are smaller than those typically found in urban high schools. Regular classes have maximum enrollment of twenty-seven students and remedial classes have a limit of fifteen students per class; the average class size is twenty.

A small school allows for a greater sense of community on the part of both students and faculty. Teachers have the students for more than one class and become more involved in helping them achieve. Teachers also help determine the school's policies and procedures, which provides them with a feeling of empowerment. Students feel that the school is theirs, and fellow students who demean the school through deviant behavior in a sense demean what belongs to them.

At LaGuardia, meeting the needs of Middle College is as important as meeting the needs of one of the academic departments of the college. Although Middle College is technically part of the board of education, for operating purposes the school is considered an integral part of the college. Any other organizational view diminishes the potential for a high school–college relationship. From its inception, the organizational structure of the two schools developed so that the needs of both institutions were in harmony.

Integration with the College Administrative Structure

The principal of Middle College is a licensed New York City Board of Education employee with the rank of principal. The individual is chosen for the post through normal board of education selection procedures that involve three screening levels before being selected by the schools chancellor. At each level, LaGuardia personnel participate and have veto power to assure that the candidate fits well into the college community. The individual selected has an informal college rank of chairperson; for all organizational and communication purposes, Middle College High

School is a department of the college. The chairpersons and academic deans meet biweekly, and the principal participates in these meetings at which academic goals, policies, and procedures are reviewed and discussed. The principal has the opportunity not only to react to issues that might affect the high school, but also to share in open discussions on all matters. Many decisions affecting everyday contact between the high school and the departments flow through this impartial relationship among administrators.

All of the chairs report directly to the dean of faculty, as does the principal of Middle College. This organizational structure sends a clear message to the college community: Middle College is a part of the college. To further integration, the Middle College calendar parallels the one used by the college, making possible more efficient use of faculty, classrooms, and laboratories by the high school.

Relationships with College Departments

Faculty of the high school are invited to teach as adjunct faculty after their regular working hours. Through teaching at the college level, the high school faculty learn about the departmental courses and standards, meet members of the department, and are invited to departmental meetings and colloquia. In addition, adjunct teaching offers a convenient way for high school teachers to supplement their income.

College faculty are offered the opportunity to teach high school-level courses as part of their regular workload or on an overload basis. Middle College receives funds from the college that are used to reimburse departments for replacement costs. Through this opportunity, faculty learn more about the educational problems facing Middle College teachers and, together with their high school colleagues, they seek possible solutions.

Student Selection Process

Understanding the nature of the program begins with the admission process, which defines the student body. Concentrating on a high-risk population, the criteria for admission are (1) a high rate of absenteeism, (2) three or more subject area failures, and (3) identified social and emotional problems stemming from the home environment. The guidance counselors of the junior high schools are asked to gather a group of students who might benefit from the Middle College program. LaGuardia Middle College staff and students visit each of the seven schools, talk to the students, and answer questions. The 140 students selected are brought in for an interview conducted by the current students at Middle College. The main purpose of this interview is to encourage the new admits to buy into the school, develop a relationship, and acquire a sense of the atmosphere. If an applicant is rejected by the students, he or she is reinterviewed. Because the student has a history of failure, it is important that he or she feels chosen for the program; therefore, the interview before acceptance is a critical part of the process to ensure that the first high school experience is a positive one. The interview allows the applicant to see that the current students are oriented toward success and that they do not see themselves as potential dropouts. The issue of personal responsibility in the midst of so much freedom is stressed, and a commitment is secured from the applicant about living up to the trust placed in him or her. At that time, he or she may be assigned a buddy or peer counselor.

In June, Middle College holds an orientation for all new students and parents, followed by a four-day orientation program during the last week of August. It includes group discussions held by student government members, a sampling of all extracurricular activities, a picnic, and color wars. In a leisurely environment, the new students meet the older ones and begin to hear about the success-oriented values of the school.

Academic Profile

Approximately 40 percent of incoming students are more than two years below grade level in reading, and about 55 percent are below grade level in mathematics. Table 1 shows the ethnic profile of the students, which has remained fairly constant over fourteen years.

Middle College maintains an enrollment of 480 students (full capacity). Small enrollment is critical not only because of limited space but because of the lack of anonymity it ensures—a necessary ingredient to develop the "family" culture of the school, as described by students. Despite the fact that the school has a population with a background of serious attendance problems, the average daily attendance is about 81 percent.

On January 9, 1983, the *New York Times* indicated that 33.9 percent of all tenth graders in New York were absent thirty times in one year; in that year at Middle College, only 13 percent of tenth graders were absent thirty times a year. In a 1980-81 study of classes, the attendance rate for Middle College was 90 percent; however, the attendance rate was almost

Table 1. Middle College Ethnic Profile

Ethnicity		Sex		Socioeconomic Status	
White	45%	Female	54%	Public Assistance	60%
Black	21%	Male	46%	Single Parents	70%
Hispanic	33%				
Asian	1%				

twice as high for students accepted from junior high school than it was for those from the high school population. One year of failure in a regular high school makes it very difficult for students to believe they can achieve.

Staff Profile

Thirty educators from regularly licensed board of education qualified lists constitute the Middle College faculty; all are teacher/counselors committed to the goals of the schools. Ninety-four percent hold master's degrees and 31 percent are in doctoral programs. Currently, a five-member faculty personnel committee interviews new candidates for a position and makes a recommendation to the principal. This hiring model follows the college hiring process more closely than the high school practice. Criteria for selection include a strong academic background and evidence of a commitment to working with students outside the classroom. The committee also identifies candidates who qualify as adjunct personnel in the college, and staff members are encouraged to take these assignments.

Career Education

LaGuardia Community College requires each day session student to complete three ten-week cooperative education internships and five ten-week quarters of study. This approach to career education allows students to link classroom and work experiences. Middle College has adopted many features of this model. Every Middle College High School student is required to complete a full- or part-time cooperative education internship during each of three years spent at the school. (Each Middle College student spends three years—tenth, eleventh, and twelfth grades—in the school, with each year divided into three trimesters or cycles.) The internships are designed to enhance students' career choices, work behavior, and understanding of vocational reward structures. Upon graduation and enrollment into LaGuardia, the secondary students receive credit for one of the three internships required for graduation from the college. The high school faculty responsible for these activities work very closely with the college's cooperative education staff. Most internships are unpaid, but students receive credit toward their high school diploma. The majority of Middle College students have full-time internships; a significant minority have part-time internships.

To facilitate the internship structure, classes typically taught in sequential fashion have been redesigned along thematically coherent patterns. For example, American Studies, a yearlong course taught in a chronological approach, has been refashioned into three distinct, nonsequential, cycle-long classes. The new courses, Government and Constitution, Cultural Pluralism, and American Foreign Policy, can be taken in any sequence, smoothing the way for the student who will be interrupting formal academic study with experiential learning.

The program propels the students and the school toward the community through an internship program that prepared each student to engage in an experiential learning activity once a year, typically in an area of community service. The Middle College high school students choose from over 350 sites in the New York City area and work in hospitals, schools, police stations, and social service agencies.

Three internship preparation courses, Personal and Career Development I and II and Decision Making, are modeled on the college's approach. Three internships, one each year, utilize and apply the teachings of each of the courses. The concepts taught in the preparation class are applied to the student's internship and reinforced by having each internship coupled with a weekly seminar. Similar to the college co-op advisement program, each student in Middle College is assigned to a career education supervisor who maintains a close relationship, both as teacher and counselor, with the student over the three years. The same faculty member serves as the student's teacher of career education courses, internship monitor, seminar leader, and career education counselor. The student and the career education supervisor decide on part- or full-time internships according to the student's readiness and competence in basic skills. Students with deficiencies in basic skills participate in part-time internships and receive remedial instruction in the early morning before going to their internship sites.

The success of Middle College students may be attributed to several elements in the internship program design:

- The three-year relationship maintained between individual students and their career education supervisors
- Careful placement of students in work environments that provide not only interesting work tasks but also coworkers and supervisors with whom students can interact positively
- Close on-site monitoring of the students by the career education supervisors
- The staff's careful development of learning sites, which includes assessment of the work site climate and needs as well as the communication of the school's goals to the work supervisor
- Reinforcement of concepts acquired by students in and out of the classroom through seminars
- The integrated nature of experiential and academic learning with mutual reinforcement
- The careful fit of internships with psychosocial needs, to providing a sense of purposefulness, pride, self-worth, and an external affirmation of students' ability to function in a world previously perceived as unrewarding, hostile, and uncaring.

For many students, the first internship provides a first school-related success. Many students receive A's from their site supervisors, in part because of realistic goal setting by student and supervisor and significant growth experienced by the fifteen- or sixteen-year-old at an external site. This part of the program turns the student's future into the present and often results in doubling the student's rate of credit accumulation per cycle. For the dropout-prone youngster, the connection between work and future as part of the school experience is a powerful tool.

Curriculum Focus

All courses are designed so students can participate in internships without falling behind. While the student is in school, he or she enrolls in double the amount of state-required courses, such as English, so that all New York State diploma requirements are met. The curricula of traditional courses like American History are divided into thirds along thematic lines. The school is not divided along the traditional lines of tenth, eleventh, and twelfth grades. Instead, each student knows how many credits he or she needs for graduation. Word processing is taught in the first career education class, and all writing projects are done on the word processor. Two computer rooms are available for students to enter drafts of assignments and to facilitate editing. The computer is also used to enhance remedial math instruction.

Most extracurricular activities usually associated with school (yearbook, newspaper, literary magazines, and plays) are performed as in-school activities. The emphasis in all classes is on project outcomes, changing the role of student from passive receptor to student as worker, editor, writer, or producer.

College/High School Staff Development

LaGuardia trains twelve teachers a year in techniques developed by the college to reinforce basic skills (reading, writing, and oral communication), while the instructors are teaching content courses. Middle College teachers participate in this training along with college teachers. The problems of teaching content courses to students with weak literacy skills are similar at both educational levels. Experience in designing courses that reinforce skills learning is essential for Middle College educators.

Availability of College Courses for Middle College Students

Having the same school calendars makes it easy for students to have access to college-level courses. Prior to the regular college registration, Middle College counselors work with their students to select the desired courses and teachers and then register the high school students. A complete list of students and courses is sent to the registrar prior to the start of college registration, and the registrar reserves the space so that students are not eliminated from any courses. The student's name appears on the class roster, and the college teacher has no way of identifying the student as a Middle College student from that document. The Middle College course program is then planned around the college class schedule. Student progress is monitored periodically by the counselor. At the end of the cycle, the counselor receives the transcripts from the registrar and enters them on the Middle College transcript.

For purposes of college records, Middle College students are considered non-degree students. They do not pay tuition of $40 per credit, which has been waived by the City University Board of Trustees. At the conclusion of the course, the student receives a grade that is placed on a regular college transcript. The transcript and credits are banked, until the time the student enrolls at LaGuardia or requests that the records be sent to another college. In order to provide a positive experience for students taking college courses, the college senate approved a policy that eliminates a failing grade. Students who do not meet the required standards are given a grade of NC or no credit. This grade does not affect the student's future grade point average. Annually, approximately eighty students take one three-credit course with a pass rate of about 66 percent. Students receive simultaneous college and high school credits for these courses. They can select from a great variety of courses from every department within the college. As a result, the Middle College curriculum is more varied, flexible, and interesting. Middle College counselors decide on the placement of students in college courses, and students may enroll in college courses based on their level of academic ability and maturity. In addition, all students must complete basic skills prerequisites as demonstrated on standardized tests such as the CUNY Freshman Skills Assessment Tests, the N.Y.C. Tests in Reading and Mathematics, and N.Y.S. Regents Competency Tests. The following criteria help identify students for college class enrollment: (1) a graduating senior who is nearing completion of his or her graduation requirements, (2) a junior or senior who has demonstrated a satisfactory academic record at Middle College, (3) a student who has satisfactorily completed the sequence of courses in a particular area (for example, a student who has completed all high school mathematics through intermediate algebra can register for college-level math), and (4) a student who has demonstrated a talent or skill in a particular area (for example, Spanish, piano, art, typing).

There are many benefits to this arrangement. From an economic point of view, it saves money for the high school by eliminating redundancy in offerings—especially in such areas as pre-calculus and languages—and by allowing for a better use of resources at the high school. This arrangement meets the needs of the gifted and talented students for advanced courses and offers every student with below or average ability the opportunity to see college as a realistic part of his or her future, thus increasing the rate at which students go on for higher education. Finally, it allows the student the opportunity to make up for time lost in high school, because of failure or truancy, without the stigma that would usually be attached to having been left back in high school.

Guidance Component

Closeness and a sense of belonging are very important to the high-risk students who, by their very definition, tend to be alienated and disenfranchised. Therefore, everyone on staff—teachers, counselors, paraprofessionals, administrators, secretaries, and security—understands his or her role as a responsible adult who can make a significant impact on the lives of the students. Students are encouraged to become involved in many ways, to reject their own irresponsible behavior, and to learn how responsible people function. This institutionalized caring is evident in the way the guidance program is structured.

Structure. While the school is small by New York City standards, Middle College is made even smaller by division into three clusters. Each cluster has a house teacher, guidance counselor, and a house mom (family workers). The clusters have seven houses with from twenty to twenty-five students. Each student stays in his or her house for the three years at Middle College so that he or she continues with the same house teacher, house mom, and guidance counselor. Monitoring a student's attendance and academic progress is the responsibility of the house teacher, in conjunction with the house mom and guidance counselor. The house teacher's task is to be the primary adult in the student's journey through high school, helping to develop individual programs for the student based on student choice, graduation requirements, academic sequence requirements and personal need—such as care of a baby, care of a sibling, or need for a job. The house teacher also monitors the student's attendance, personally calling each one after two days of absence.

Group Activities. Students in each cluster who experience difficulty— that is, poor attendance, cutting, or academic failure—are recommended for group counseling. There are ten daily group counseling sessions usually involving about 140 students, almost one-third of the school. The group is designed to help the student develop coping strategies that will enable his or her adjustment to difficult home situations or to the onerous challenges involved in adolescent development. Experience over the years has shown the group process to be the most efficient and effective way to deliver guidance services. Open peer discussion in a climate of mutual trust and freedom of expression reduces defensiveness and allows each group member to move toward acceptance of who he or she is emotionally, intellectually and physically and to realize the possibility of attaining new goals. Devoting time during the school day to these issues allows students to realize the relationship between self-esteem and better academic achievement. A study conducted in June 1986, reported that 84 percent of the participants in group counseling achieved more credits while in counseling than they did in the cycle before placement in the group. Additionally, students who withdrew prematurely from group counseling declined in their rate of credit accumulation.

Parental Support Group. The parent support group, which meets monthly at Middle College, is an outgrowth of group counseling. Parents having difficulty with their children expressed interest in meeting regularly to gain insight into and support for good parenting of their adolescents. The support group is conducted by a male and a female counselor so that both mothers and fathers feel free to join and to express feelings. The counselors follow the agenda set by the parents, using guest experts as needed. Those parents who participate gain strategies for dealing with difficult teenagers and acquire support for this most difficult period of parenthood.

Peer Counseling. For many years, Middle College has had a comprehensive peer counseling program, originally modeled after a similar program at LaGuardia Community College. Each year twenty students, recommended by teachers and current peer counselors, are trained in micro-counseling techniques for two periods a day. Once they are certified, these students then interview incoming students, acquire a caseload of students, and conduct internships in places where their skills are used, such as community-based drug programs in Middle College or in local schools. As in all peer programs, the value lies in the increased self-esteem and communication skills for the peer counselor as well as the help given to the student in trouble.

Student Government

Students have written a detailed constitution that governs student behavior, rights, and responsibilities. Each cycle, students from each house who are in good academic standing are elected to student government. They meet daily to decide the student activity budget, to plan and coordinate school activities, and to hold student/faculty peer review. Students are referred to student government for a number of reasons, including behavior that is disruptive to the learning community. Answering to one's peers is a powerful way to change negative behavior. The students refer to this as "the power of the peer," and constant attention is paid to using this power positively.

Results

The dropout rate for the Middle College has consistently remained lower than that of the average high school in New York City. Over the years, the attrition rate has averaged about 15 percent, supporting the original hypothesis that a cooperative relationship between a high school and a college can effectively improve retention. Some 72 percent of the graduates go on to college, 22 percent become employed, and 4 percent enter the military. Of those who go on to college, 82 percent remain in the City University of New York system, 12 percent attend New York State colleges, and 6 percent attend private institutions; LaGuardia receives about 27 percent of those who go on to college. Additionally, some students go out to work first before they return to attend LaGuardia. Approximately half the students who go on to higher education attend a four-year college, and half attend a two-year college.

In a follow-up study of the graduates at the time of the tenth anniversary of the school, 20 percent responded to a questionnaire. Based on that data, 75 percent had, in fact, gone on to college, with 76 percent of that number having completed one year's worth of credits. Of those who went on to work, 51 percent reported earning $10 or more per hour in a skilled job category.

The Future

The New York State Legislature recognized the involvement of community colleges in close collaboration with high schools in helping solve the dropout problem. With the governor's support, funds were made available for the replication of Middle College High School at LaGuardia Community College. Middle colleges were created at Brooklyn College, Bronx Community College, Hostos Community College, and a second middle college at LaGuardia was established to serve the needs of recent immigrants. With the help of the Ford Foundation, middle colleges have been established in Memphis, Tennessee, Peoria, Illinois, and Union County, New Jersey. Chicago has developed two middle colleges since September 1985.

Eleven high schools are currently operating in conjunction with a two- or four-year college, and at least nine additional middle colleges are being planned across the nation. Class collaboration between high schools and colleges is beginning to be an important approach to dropout prevention.

Cecilia Cullen is principal of Middle College High School at LaGuardia Community College.

Martin G. Moed, vice-president and dean of faculty at LaGuardia Community College, has been the college administrator responsible for supervising the Middle College program. In this capacity, he represents the collaborative within the college and within the City University of New York's overarching structure.

Colleges continue to provide the same traditional learning settings and structures to all students, despite the fact that the settings are often unsuccessful with young high-risk students. Learning communities, skills across the curriculum, and work experience programs offer hope for engaging high-risk students in the learning process.

Helping Students Learn

Anne-Marie McCartan

Lisa, who graduated from high school last spring, decides at the last minute to enroll at the local community college for classes in the fall. Although only a fair student in high school, she did graduate, unlike several of her friends. She hopes to be a nurse but wanted a year off after high school to earn money to buy a car. Since she could find only part-time work as an aide at a nursing home, she decides to get a start on college.

Lisa shows up on Thursday of registration week and is told that she needs to take placement tests in English and mathematics before choosing her classes. After taking the tests, she is advised to enroll in what the college calls developmental writing and reading before attempting English 101. Since the catalogue says she will need biology for the nursing program, she signs up for Biology I, Developmental Writing, and Introduction to Psychology. She is to report for Psychology on Monday morning at 10:00 A.M. Before then, she will have to rearrange her hours at the nursing home, since she is now scheduled to work in the mornings.

How will Lisa fare in her first semester at college? Lisa is typical of one profile of high-risk community college students. She is:
- academically underprepared
- undermotivated for college
- poorly informed (and perhaps unrealistic) about her career goals
- employed off-campus
- young.

What does this imply for the learning needs Lisa will bring to the classroom? Lisa's psychology professor provides a good lens through which to view this question. The professor is trained in the content area but not in pedagogy—particularly not in how to teach underprepared students. She will be faced with a classroom of students possessing a wide range of skill levels: those like Lisa, with pre-collegiate writing skills; returning adults who have recently passed the GED; and students with solid academic preparation. Moreover, the professor must wait until the semester progresses to learn which students fall into which of these categories (Simms, 1984).

Lisa's teacher will have to decide how to deal with the fact that Lisa could not rearrange her work schedule until the second week of classes and therefore missed the first two class sessions. She will be unsure whether or not to correct Lisa's grammar or if doing so would hinder Lisa's desire to participate and learn. The professor will be inclined to give multiple-choice examinations because the course has no prerequisites and many students are not writing at the college level.

Must this be the scenario? The challenges for both student and teacher to make college a success are great. Are we destined to keep our fingers crossed for Lisa and her peers until some greater force improves the situation?

Much attention has been given to the need to restructure educational systems and offerings to better serve the older adult learner. Although many community colleges report a high median age (usually around twenty-seven years) of students, post-high school age individuals comprise roughly one-third of most colleges' student populations. We may have diverted too much attention away from the needs of underprepared eighteen-year-olds who are making what may be a traumatic transition from high school to college.

The odds are against Lisa's successfully completing an associate degree program. Yet we offer Lisa the same learning structure—three classes, each meeting three times a week, with independent homework assignments—that we offer the most capable, self-directed entering college freshman. This chapter presents several alternatives to traditional first-semester experiences that have shown promise for high-risk students. The common thread in these approaches is that each uses existing resources and opportunities to make the initial college term a successful learning experience for Lisa and her peers and a gratifying teaching experience for her professors.

Forming Community

Surprisingly, the initial risk of failure that Lisa confronts is not academic. Because a student can continue to attend college even while failing, Lisa is not likely to leave college solely for academic reasons before the completion of the term.

The major risk for Lisa is that she will never become engaged in her studies and consequently will begin to miss classes, falling further and further behind. Because she has three different professors and three groups of students who sit alongside her in class, only the registrar may know whether or not Lisa completes the semester. Where, at a community college, can Lisa develop the kinds of relationships with her peers and professors that she would be able to had she attended a four-year residential college? Presumably, commuter students have no less inherent need to form communities and engage in comradeship than students who leave home for college. Indeed, Katz (1985) has identified "lack of collaborative learning" as one of three major obstacles to student learning. (Katz sees the other two obstacles as being lack of individualization and lack of opportunity for applying ideas to situations in which the student has responsibility.) Consequently, several colleges have attempted to offer students the opportunity for community through various kinds of learning groups.

Bouton and Garth champion this approach in their book, *Learning in Groups*, and see the term as encompassing a variety of activities, including collaborative learning, study circles, peer support groups, and work groups. All seem to have two major elements: first, a process of group conversation and activity that promotes active learning; second, a way for faculty to guide this learning process and to offer expertise by structuring tasks or activities (1983a, p. 2). Prominent examples include the problem-centered approach to medical education pioneered by McMaster University, the Weekend Learning Community for working adults at Lesley College, Washington State's Evergreen College, and Delta College of SUNY College at Brockport. Learning groups have proven successful in helping students improve their writing (Bruffee, 1983; Elsbree, 1985), in training graduate students in the humanities to collaborate with their colleagues (Maimon, 1983), and in providing a framework for persons with similar interests to approach a concern, solve a problem, or learn more about a specific issue in the community as opposed to in the classroom (Osborne, 1983).

Recently, several community colleges have expanded on this notion to form what are called *learning communities*. Students with similar academic preparation and learning needs are typically block-programmed for a prescribed course of study based on their needs and interests. A learning community for Lisa might look something like this: She and twenty-four other students report to the same room Monday through Friday at 8:30 in the morning. Two professors, one an English teacher, the other a member of the psychology faculty, have teamed up to offer nine credits under the theme "Psychology in Everyday Life." A college counselor joins the group each day for the first hour. With clear direction and monitoring by the instructors, students will spend much of the time working in small study groups. Upon successful completion of the course, Lisa will be awarded three credits in psychology and six credits in developmental reading and writing, and she will be prepared to enter English 101.

Such a learning community provides several solutions to the problems that plague high-risk high school graduates entering a community college. First, the learning community offers students repeated contact with a peer group, which can lead to friendships and social support networks. Formation of social bonds can encourage persistence in college. In a learning community, it is difficult for a student to vanish from college; teachers and other students notice absences from the group and will attempt to track down a missing student.

Second, the learning community encourages active, involved learning since it "engages students in a learning process that enables them both to acquire a knowledge of the material and to develop their skills in the process of acquiring that knowledge" (Bouton and Rice, 1983, p. 32). Students continually are afforded opportunities to practice interpersonal, problem-solving, and communication skills in the small study groups. Bouton and Garth believe that "communication in learning groups is enhanced because all participants are relatively close to one another in stage of development and level of understanding. By contrast, faculty and students are often at such different levels of understanding that they talk past each other" (1983b, p. 78).

Third, the presence of a counselor provides a direct link with an array of services available through student development programs. An astute counselor will learn to recognize particular needs of individual students and direct them to appropriate services. Likewise, students learn to know and trust the counselor, becoming less reluctant than the typical freshman to approach a counselor with academic or personal problems or for educational or career guidance.

Finally, learning communities that allow a maximum of interaction and time spent between teacher and student encourage the conditions found to enhance effective relationships between students and teachers (Wilson and others, 1975; Chickering and Gamson, 1987). Chickering and Gamson believe that "knowing a few faculty members well enhances students' intellectual commitment and encourages them to think about their own values and future plans" (1987, p. 4).

Despite the potential benefits, learning communities place considerable new responsibilities on both parties of the learning process, particularly on students. "Students are faced with new levels of responsibility for what happens in the classroom," acknowledge Bouton and Garth. "They are inexperienced in working with their fellow students, and consequently they are ineffective. They have difficulty giving and receiving criticism, maintaining their own focus on the task, and acknowledging and resolving the inevitable conflicts that arise in cooperative work" (1983b, p. 81).

Those who have conscientiously striven to overcome the traditional social relations of the classroom through learning groups speak of them with almost unbridled optimism. Yet, one of the movement's most ardent enthusiasts and practitioners, Kenneth Bruffee, points out that to date there is not much research on the effects of collaborative learning in colleges and universities (Bruffee, 1987, p. 44). More systematic data offering evidence of its benefits is needed before learning communities will build much momentum in community colleges.

Skills Across the Curriculum

The hypothetical learning community described earlier also provides the opportunity for another approach to helping students such as Lisa persist and learn in college: the teaching of basic skills across the curriculum. Researchers find that basic skills are learned best when taught through content. A developmental writing course is unlikely to affect Lisa's performance in and understanding of psychology if taken during the same semester as but not integrated with her psychology course. Lisa's psychology professor will see few improvements in Lisa's written work during the course of the semester. Teaching basic skills apart from content is a process that apparently ill-served Lisa in high school. As a high school graduate with passing marks in English, she comes to college lacking college-level skills in reading and writing. If the separate course approach did not work for her already, why would it work for her in college? Combining the two courses enables her to improve her English skills and enhances her ability to comprehend psychology.

Skills across the curriculum have proved successful in settings other than learning communities. The most common examples are the writing across the curriculum programs that have become features of many undergraduate colleges. Colleges also have introduced critical thinking, reading, listening, and problem solving across the curriculum. Although approaches vary widely, all seem to share the notion that basic skills (writing, reading, thinking) are not discrete entities but processes; basic skills are not merely things to learn but ways of communicating and learning (see interview with Elaine Maimon in Smith, 1983-84). Less emphasis is placed on finding the right answer than on the process of focusing and developing the answers. In colleges that implement a skill across the curriculum, faculty in English (or philosophy, in the case of critical thinking) must give more attention to the subjects students study, and faculty in other departments must give more attention to the identified skill (Graham, 1983-84).

Despite the well-publicized benefits of skills-across-the-curriculum programs, few community colleges have adopted this approach wholesale. What are possible reasons for this reluctance?

As with four-year college faculty, integration of writing and other skills into content curriculum often takes considerable work on the part of the faculty. Such a commitment is particularly unlikely from part-time faculty, who number more than half the total faculty in community colleges. Faculty development programs are still poorly defined for two-year college faculty, with most programs consisting of discipline-based institutes, released time, and sabbatical leaves (Cohen and Brawer, 1982, p. 71).

Full-time faculty in disciplines, despite their belief in the community college mission, often are reluctant to take responsibility for students' skill development needs. They are satisfied to leave remedial teaching to specialists, those trained in and hired by the college to address this level of need. In all fairness, most teachers would be unable to supply the necessary assistance without considerable in-service training. With teaching loads averaging four classes a term, few faculty are able to commit the necessary time to develop new teaching skills. Colleges are often disinclined to grant released time for this purpose.

In addition, most colleges have been unwilling, for a variety of reasons, to require that students complete developmental coursework prior to enrolling in college-level courses. That is, most colleges do not establish English 101 as a prerequisite or even corequisite for enrollment in most general education courses.

How might community colleges circumvent these problems? Team teaching seems a better approach than having teachers individually incorporate skills into content. Defining the task as team teaching rather than interdisciplinary teaching may help, since team-taught courses need not be interdisciplinary (White, 1981). Interdisciplinarity, White contends, "depends on the existence of a point of view toward the subject matter and toward knowledge in general" (p. 6). Such an expectation, while desirable, is not required of community college faculty who are contemplating joining forces to teach an introductory social science or humanities course. Requisites are (1) a desire to help students learn a subject by helping them improve their communication skills (particularly reading and writing), (2) a true spirit of cooperation between participating faculty, and (3) time to carefully plan the course, at least prior to offering it for the first time.

Sherman and Taylor (1982, pp. 67-68) describe two models for this to take place. The first model is an integrated course, in which a skills course and content course are offered in tandem for the combined credit that each would give separately. The authors use the examples of a community college where students can register simultaneously for both Fundamentals of Reading and Writing and Introductory Psychology. The second model is the team teacher course, in which content and process are fully woven together. In both model courses, a skills specialist and a content-based instructor work together to equip students with basic skills, "those communication and learning skills that an individual needs to carry out specific academic, career, or broader life tasks" (p. 62).

Linking Work with Learning

A universal truth about community college students is that they work while going to school. Lisa will more likely quit school than quit work if she finds herself unable to do both simultaneously. Her work schedule is likely to be a primary criterion by which she chooses the courses she will take.

Community colleges have made several concessions to these realities. Most classes are scheduled for mornings, late afternoons, and evenings; learning resource centers and counseling centers are open after 5:00 P.M.; and homework assignments may be lighter than those required of students in residential colleges. But often the fact that students work provokes a shoulder-shrugging, "What can we do?" attitude from college personnel, rather than attempts to explore creative ways to build upon that fact.

Cooperative education programs are the most coherent and successful attempt at linking jobs with learning experiences. The virtues of cooperative education programs have been extolled often by those, including Duley (1978, p. 320), who believe their primary benefit "is the application and integration of knowledge and the acquisition of skills necessary to an educated and mature person." In Chapter Ten of this volume, E. B. Kirkbride describes a successful program that offers high school students in computers, office systems, electronics, and nursing programs the opportunity for advanced standing and cooperative education in the community college. Community colleges also sponsor programs such as internships, externships, and clinical experiences associated with vocational-technical programs.

Unfortunately, little research has been conducted on the usefulness of work experience programs to students' career development needs (Sexton and Ungerer, 1975). However, a content analysis of intensive interviews conducted with community college students about what most influenced their educational and career decision making while in college (McCartan, 1986) suggests that the opportunity for work experience related to a student's chosen or tentative career choice is significant. Further analysis of the interviews reveals the following ways in which students feel they benefit from these experiences:

1. *Career choice.* Having a career-related job experience while in col-

lege helped several students verify that the career they had chosen was right for them. Students like Lisa who had little or no prior work experience found career-related job experience particularly important.

2. *Career specialization.* Work experience related to a student's chosen career served less as a way of exploring a chosen field than as a way of helping them identify what they would like to specialize in within that field. By the time most students participate in a sponsored work experience, particularly co-op, they have already settled on a major and have a fairly defined career choice in mind.

3. *Career options.* Fewer students found that work experience helped them explore a tentative career choice. For the few students who did find jobs helpful in trying out a career, these jobs were not part of an organized program. They found these jobs on their own early in their college years.

4. *Skills or credentials needed.* Through work experience related to a chosen field, students often find out they are not adequately skilled or credentialed to progress up the ladder in their field. Several students interviewed became convinced that they should stay in college and finish their associate degree, even though completion was not a requirement of their profession. Some students raised their degree aspirations to pursue the baccalaureate when they began to see its importance in the workplace.

Without detracting from the significant benefits of cooperative education programs, other ways may exist to help link students' need to work with an opportunity for learning to occur. Although some students use cooperative education for career exploration, many students are committed to their chosen career, and the experience serves more as an opportunity for clarification and specification than for exploration. What good is a cooperative experience for young, high-risk students like Lisa when it occurs well along in an academic or occupational program?

In the absence of formal internship, co-op, or clinical experience programs, students will nonetheless seek out work that is related to their chosen or considered career choice. So, while students' outside jobs often are considered a major cause of student attrition, such attrition may be due to the fact that those jobs have not been integrated with students' educational programs adequately or early enough. Rather than ignoring the important learning that appears to be going on in outside jobs, colleges can employ strategies to integrate these jobs into the formal learning process. Along with full-fledged internship and cooperative education programs, community colleges should offer students in related outside jobs the option of gaining credit for this experience. Students could be assisted in defining learning objectives, and credit could be contingent upon attendance at a seminar where issues of the workplace are discussed, as they are in co-op seminars. This allows students who find jobs on their own to reflect on and receive feedback to use in building on their experience-based knowledge. As van Aalst argues (1979, p. 36), "Adding a learning component to . . . existing low-level jobs is easier than designing an equal number of new experiential educational positions." Faculty in all disciplines can attempt to learn about the jobs held by their students and then weave those experiences into class discussions, lectures, and assignments. Students are not working solely to make money; if possible, they will try to get a job that helps them move toward a career goal. The more that colleges can do to transform students' jobs into learning experiences, the less likely it will be that the college will lose out to jobs if a student feels he or she must make a choice between the two.

Lisa's job in the nursing home presents her instructors with a marvelous opportunity to help her explore her motivation and capabilities for a career in nursing, understand the career ladders in the field, and realize the qualifications necessary for the various levels and specialties. Activities to gain this knowledge might include a research project, interviews with allied health professionals, or an investigation of alternative career choices in the health care field.

This chapter has offered three suggestions for improving the chances that young, high-risk students like Lisa will continue to the second semester and beyond at community colleges. All suggestions involve ways to engage students in the learning process: designing experiences that promote meaningful interaction with others, integrating basic skills with content curriculum, and recognizing the need to work and go to college at the same time.

References

Bouton, C., and Garth, R. Y. (eds.). *Learning in Groups*. New Directions for Teaching and Learning, no. 14. San Francisco: Jossey-Bass, 1983a.

Bouton, C., and Garth, R. Y. "Students in Learning Groups: Active Learning Through Conversation." In C. Bouton and R. Y. Garth (eds.), *Learning in Groups*. New Directions for Teaching and Learning, no. 14. San Francisco: Jossey-Bass, 1983b.

Bouton, C., and Rice, B. "Developing Student Skills and Abilities." In C. Bouton and R. Y. Garth (eds.), *Learning in Groups*. New Directions for Teaching and Learning, no. 14. San Francisco: Jossey-Bass, 1983.

Bruffee, K. A. "Teaching Writing Through Collaboration." In C. Bouton and R. Y. Garth (eds.), *Learning in Groups*. New Directions for Teaching and Learning, no. 14. San Francisco: Jossey-Bass, 1983.

Bruffee, K. A. "The Art of Collaborative Learning." *Change*, 1987, *19* (2), 42-47.

Chickering, A. W., and Gamson, Z. F. "Seven Principles for Good Practice in Undergraduate Education." *American Association for Higher Education Bulletin*, 1987, *39* (7), 3-7.

Cohen, A. M., and Brawer, F. B. *The American Community College*. San Francisco: Jossey-Bass, 1982.

Duley, J. S. "Learning Through Field Experience." In O. Milton and Associates (eds.), *On College Teaching: A Guide to Contemporary Practices.* San Francisco: Jossey-Bass, 1978.

Elsbree, L. "Learning to Write Through Mutual Coaching." In J. Katz (ed.), *Teaching as Though Students Mattered.* New Directions for Teaching and Learning, no. 21. San Francisco: Jossey-Bass, 1985.

Graham, J. "What Works: The Problems and Rewards of Cross-Curriculum Writing Programs." In B. L. Smith (ed.), *Writing Across the Curriculum.* Current Issues in Higher Education, no. 3. Washington, D.C.: American Association for Higher Education, 1983-84.

Katz, J. (ed.). *Teaching as Though Students Mattered.* New Directions for Teaching and Learning, no. 21. San Francisco: Jossey-Bass, 1985.

McCartan, A. M. "Student Career Decision Making: Influential Variables in Community Colleges." Unpublished doctoral dissertation, Harvard Graduate School of Education, 1986.

Maimon, E. P. "Graduate Education and Cooperative Scholarship." In C. Bouton and R. Y. Garth (eds.), *Learning in Groups.* New Directions for Teaching and Learning, no. 14. San Francisco: Jossey-Bass, 1983.

Osborne, K. Q. "Learning Beyond the Classroom." In C. Bouton and R. Y. Garth (eds.), *Learning in Groups.* New Directions for Teaching and Learning, no. 14. San Francisco: Jossey-Bass, 1983.

Sexton, R. F., and Ungerer, R. A. *Rationales for Experiential Education.* ERIC/ Higher Education Research Report, no. 3. Washington, D.C.: American Association for Higher Education, 1975.

Sherman, D., and Taylor, C. "Basic Skills for the Diversely Prepared." In C. Taylor (ed.), *Diverse Student Population: Benefits and Issues.* New Directions for Experiential Learning, no. 17. San Francisco: Jossey-Bass, 1982.

Simms, R. B. "Accommodating the Remedial Student in the Content Classroom." *Improving College and University Teaching,* 1984, *32* (4), 195-199.

Smith, B. L. "An Interview with Elaine Maimon." In B. L. Smith (ed.), *Writing Across the Curriculum.* Current Issues in Higher Education, no. 3. Washington, D.C.: American Association for Higher Education, 1983-84.

van Aalst, F. D. "Career Development Theory and Practice." In F. D. van Aalst (ed.), *Combining Career Development with Experiential Learning.* New Directions for Experiential Learning, no. 5. San Francisco: Jossey-Bass, 1979.

White, A. M. (ed.). *Interdisciplinary Teaching.* New Directions for Teaching and Learning, no. 8. San Francisco: Jossey-Bass, 1981.

Wilson, R. C., and others. *College Professors and Their Impact on Students.* New York: Wiley, 1975.

Anne-Marie McCartan is coordinator for academic programs at the State Council of Higher Education for Virginia. Previously she served as director of the transfer opportunities program at Roxbury Community College in Boston.

The College Orientation Program demonstrates what community colleges can do to orient high-risk students to college before high school graduation.

Reaching Students: Communication from the Community Colleges

Elizabeth A. Warren

> It made me think twice about school. It made me realize how important college is.

> It has helped me relax when I think of college. It got rid of a lot of myths I believed in. I'm not as scared as I was.

The students quoted above were seniors in Phoenix high schools last year and had just completed the College Orientation Program. During the last two years, over 500 minority and low-income high school seniors have come to South Mountain Community College to participate in a three-day intensive orientation program for one hour of college credit. Many students who have attended the orientation might not otherwise ever set foot on a college campus.

The student quotes capture the essence of why the program was created: to familiarize new or prospective students with the college environment, to reduce their anxiety about college, to encourage them to continue their education, and to provide them with skills that will be beneficial to them in high school and beyond. College faculty counselors—who have the skill and sensitivity necessary to work with high-risk, potentially first-generation college students—teach the orientations.

The College Orientation Program was developed in 1983 as the first phase of the Transfer Opportunities Program, a Ford Foundation-funded effort designed to increase the numbers of minority and low-income students who successfully transfer from community colleges to four-year colleges and universities. The orientation functions as the first link in a supportive chain of three programs that provide assistance to students as they enter college, increase retention through their college coursework, and improve orientation and transfer rates to a four-year college or university.

The target groups for the orientation include students who are new to the college and have been assessed as ready for college-level work, and students who are entering college-level work from the basic skills and English-as-a-second-language programs. A special format was designed for high school seniors in the belief that in order to have a significant impact on the transfer rate of minority and low-income students from community college to university, the college must also be concerned about the transfer rate of students from high school to community college. Our intent was to expose students to postsecondary education in general, including universities, and to South Mountain Community College in particular. We hoped that by introducing students to college during the three-day orientation they would not only seriously consider continuing their education, but also acquire skills, incentives, and motivation to remain in high school until graduation.

Encouraged by a commitment from a local foundation to provide the tuition for any high school student who attended the orientation, we first approached St. Mary's High School, an inner-city parochial school with a high percentage of minority students. We presented the program curriculum and schedule to the school's principal and counselor, anticipating they would allow fifteen or twenty seniors to attend the orientation.

To our surprise, the principal elected to send the entire senior class of approximately sixty students. The first College Orientation Program for high school students was held for the senior class of St. Mary's High School in the spring of 1985. The program has since grown to include five local high schools, all with high percentages of minority and low-income students. More than 200 students are enrolled each year in the program.

Description of the Program

> I have learned and realized the seriousness of studying, notes, and time management. I've learned some tips that will help me to do better on exams and how to handle problems and stress that go along with college.

> The most helpful subject we covered during the three-day preparation for college program was learning how to take my tests without stressing my brain too much.

Study skills, coping skills, assessment, and exposure to postsecondary education are the themes of the College Orientation Program. The orientation is based on a one-credit counseling course called Orientation for Student Development. A member of the counseling faculty at the college designed the original curriculum for the course; later, the same counselor and a counselor from one of the participating high schools refined the curriculum for the high school program.

The curriculum is organized into fourteen modules from which high schools make selections. The modules are grouped by orientation theme: study skills, coping skills, assessment, and exposure to postsecondary education. The note taking, test taking, and assessment and advisement modules that take up approximately half the orientation are not negotiable, but the remaining time can be scheduled to meet the needs of the particular high school. For example, if a high school has a computer lab to which their students have had wide exposure, they are not likely to choose the module that orients the students to the college's computer lab.

Study Skills Modules. The purpose of the five study skills modules—Study Skills, Note Taking, Test Taking, Computer Usage, and Library Usage—is to acquaint students with the skills they will need in college and can also apply while still in high school. Current study skills are assessed, and examples of effective habits are elicited from the group. Students are then taught at least one system for taking notes, common symbols and abbreviations used in note taking, and how to listen for key information. To practice these skills, students either sit in on a class in progress, or a college faculty member comes to them to deliver a short lecture.

Effectively studying from notes leads into study techniques for both objective and essay tests. Short essay and objective tests are given for practice. This practice is most effective when a test can be generated from the faculty lecture in the note taking module, thus reinforcing the connection between note taking and test taking. Schools can also choose to include modules on library and computer usage. The lab technician and the librarian usually teach these modules.

Coping Skills. These coping skills modules—Stress Reduction, Time Management, and Success and You in College—are interspersed with the study skills modules to reinforce the connection between effective self-management and success in education. Students are acquainted with both the psychological and physiological signs of stress and strategies for reducing stress, in particular effective time management. Students plot their current use of time, as well as potential schedules that build in course work and study commitments. Reading college schedules and the differences between high school and college scheduling are also discussed here.

Most important, students are taught that success in the higher education system is linked to maintaining positive attitudes and behavior. The importance of a positive attitude in easing the transition from high school to college is stressed. This module is often used to close the orientation as students are taken through a guided imagery exercise in which they imagine a positive and successful experience for themselves at college.

Assessment. These three assessment modules—College Assessment and Advisement, Learning Styles, and Career Interest Survey—provide students with some baseline information about themselves to use as they plan their education. Students are assessed in English and mathematics and reading, using the college's standard assessment instruments. Their scores are interpreted individually when possible so that students understand the implications of their scores in relation to the level of courses they should take. Students are also advised individually to spare them any embarrassment in the event of low scores.

In this module, the counseling context of the orientation and the presence of the faculty counselor are critical. If not properly handled, interpreting assessment scores can cause students to become disillusioned about their chances for success or to consider unrealistic expectations. The college assessment and advisement module is mandatory.

Students can also be given learning style and career interest surveys. Knowledge of personal learning style is applied to effective study habits for each individual. Results of career interest surveys are integrated with potential courses of study. The importance of selecting a career goal and its relation to the likelihood of completing a degree program is emphasized.

Exposure to Postsecondary Education. The three modules in this category—College Selection, College Terminology, and Support Services—utilize materials and speakers from the college and the state universities. The intent is exposure to a broad range of institutions combined with encouragement to continue past high school. Criteria for choosing the college or university that best suits individual students are discussed. Students become acquainted with the terminology of higher education and how it differs from terms used in high school. The basic offices and services that students can expect to find on most college and university campuses are described. Representatives from the more important offices such as financial aid often speak during this module.

Program Operation

> It was very well structured and all of it was very well rounded.

> The instructor was nice and answered any and all questions. She tried to find out answers for us. Also she was very interesting.

Operating a successful orientation program requires effective organization, planning, and careful selection and preparation of teachers. The first step is contacting the high school and selecting the dates for the orientation. If the school has not participated before, the program is explained to the principal and counselors. High school counselors usually work with the college to decide which modules should be included in the orientation. The high school and college also agree on the selection of students and their transportation to the college. Program staff usually go to the high school to register the students, which also provides an opportunity to prepare the students for the experience. Questions from students usually include what they can wear, how old the college students are, and where they can eat.

After the high school has committed to a date, the orientation is scheduled and guest speakers and services are confirmed. As more students and more sections are added, the scheduling gets increasingly complicated since the same speakers are often needed in each section. Services such as the bookstore and food service are also alerted since their operations are directly affected by an influx of students.

Approximately one week before the orientation, the entire college faculty and staff are notified that a group of high school students will be on campus for a three-day orientation. Preparing the college for the students is important in assuring that the students are well received. The college must be receptive to the students, since comfort with the institution is a major objective of the orientation.

The selection and preparation of teachers is probably the most critical factor in terms of the students' perception of the success of the orientation. Since the orientation is a one-credit counseling course, faculty must be certified to teach counseling within the community colleges. Faculty who have had experience with younger students and with minority and low-income students must be chosen. Faculty are sought who are engaging and energetic. Although the faculty counselors do not teach every module, they serve to coordinate the experience for the students and to establish a positive environment through group support and rapport. The faculty counselors are at the center of the orientation, connecting and coordinating the experience for students.

In preparation for the orientation, faculty receive a curriculum guide that outlines each module, lists the handouts and other resources available on the topic, and suggests related courses offered by the institution. Faculty receive occasional training on note taking and test taking from English or reading faculty to better prepare them in these areas. Faculty select from existing materials or provide the materials and handouts they wish to use in each module. These handouts are then duplicated and arranged in individual packets for each student.

The orientations are usually scheduled from 8:30 A.M. to 1:30 P.M. on

Tuesday, Wednesday, and Thursday with half an hour for lunch. Sometime during the first day, the college president or another top-ranking college official greets the students. Representatives from the foundation that provides their tuition may also visit the students. On the last day, students evaluate the program. These results, from which the quotations cited at the beginning of each section have been chosen, are shared with the faculty, college, and high school administration. The results are used to shape and modify the orientation. For example, after an early orientation, students suggested that they would like to sit in on actual classes, and this feature was subsequently added.

Interinstitutional Collaboration

> It gave me a great opportunity to actually experience what college is all about. I think the note taking, computers, and test taking were very interesting.
>
> You gave us a basic idea of what to expect when we go to college.
>
> It gave me some encouragement in succeeding in college. . . . It helped me to be more confident about college.

Exposure to college can reduce students' anxiety or uncertainty about continuing after high school. For students to experience a bridge between institutions, the institutions must formulate tangible links, such as the orientation program. The College Orientation Program's effectiveness hinged on a four-way collaboration between high schools, community college, universities, and private foundations.

Private Foundations. Support from the Ford Foundation allowed the college to develop and administer the program. Support from the Dougherty Foundation, a private local foundation, allowed the college to serve its target group of low-income and minority students by providing the tuition for any student who enrolled in the program. The Dougherty Foundation has taken a very personal and direct interest in the students in the program, who are eligible for later support from the foundation. Foundation members often visit orientations in progress to meet students and apprise them of future available scholarship and loan opportunities.

High Schools. High school counselors and principals work closely with the college to inform students and staff about the program. The high schools generally take the full responsibility to recruit students for the program and transport the students to and from the college. They also make all arrangements with students' parents and with the teachers whose classes the students will miss.

Universities. The three state universities have taken a very active role in the orientation by sending university counselors, admission officers, and recruiters to serve as guest speakers. University personnel most frequently address sections on college and university life and on how to select a college.

College. The college provides the overall context in which the orientation takes place. Because the college is small and the orientations are frequently large, offering the program involves the whole campus, from faculty to food service.

The program would not be functional, and certainly not as interesting or effective, without the collaboration from all four sectors. When institutions that normally function sequentially can operate simultaneously toward a common goal, students' perception of the gaps between the educational levels can be significantly reduced.

Future Plans

> This program was extremely helpful and should continue for all high school students across the country. I think it should be adopted by more universities also.
>
> I strongly suggest that students from all high schools be involved in an activity such as this.
>
> Keep up the program. I really honestly enjoyed every minute of it.

Colleges and universities across the nation are realizing the importance of providing a comprehensive orientation experience for their students. Important results of the College Orientation Program have been the college's scheduling more sections of the program, as well as making the orientation program longer and more inclusive.

In addition to making the orientation experience more meaningful for students at the college, South Mountain is interested in exposing students to college earlier in their high school careers. Based on the success of the College Orientation Program, the college is developing a program that will recruit students in their sophomore year and involve them and their parents with the college during both their junior and senior years. The intent is to provide students an even greater opportunity to become familiar with the college, as well as to develop the skills they will need to be successful.

Elizabeth A. Warren is coordinator of research and development at South Mountain Community College in Phoenix, Arizona. She was the original director of the Transfer Opportunities Program and is currently working on a program to increase the number of high-risk students who successfully earn baccalaureate degrees after completing high school and community college degrees.

Research on three urban school programs shows average achievers may succeed in college courses. Data encourages more outreach.

High School Students in College Courses: Three Programs

Arthur Richard Greenberg

Background

College-level study in high school has long been the exclusive province of high-achieving students. Historically students with low to moderate levels of achievement have not had the opportunity to take college-level work in high school.

Nevertheless, students who enter college after high school graduation represent a broad cross section of ability. Recent data underscore this point: Some 2,650,000 students graduated from high schools in the United States in June 1985 (Rothman, 1986). In September 1985, approximately 50 percent of those students entered 2,100 two-year and four-year colleges (Boyer, 1987, p. 1). If one assumes that every student in the top decile of the graduating class attended college, then more than one million low to moderate achievers also attended. Historical trends show that despite the inclusion of these lower-performing students, this entering class maintains a mean grade point average of C+ during freshman year (Ramist, 1984, p. 163).

Many students who graduate from high school go on to college three months later and succeed, even though they were not part of the highest-achieving group in secondary school. Acknowledgement of these conditions prompts two questions: Why are these students generally excluded from earning college credit while in high school? What happens when these students are permitted to take credit-bearing college courses in high school?

Reasons for Exclusion: Concurrent Enrollment

Concurrent (or dual) enrollment occurs when high school students enroll in college-level classes for simultaneous high school and college credit (Kleinrock, 1986). While many variations on the concurrent enrollment theme exist, Wilbur and Chapman (1978, p. 9–11) offer four general models, amended in Table 1, that reflect implementation on either the high school or college campus.

In this matrix, models A and B involve regular college faculty who teach either regular college courses (model B) or adapted college courses (model A), while models C and D represent, respectively, adapted college courses and regular college courses taught by high school faculty. Depending on individual arrangements, both course designs may be taught on either the college campus (*) or the high school campus (+).

This model can be used to identify the articulation approaches used by the three local programs studied. City-As-School and Middle College utilize design B* (regular college faculty, regular catalog courses, taught on the college campus). College Now utilizes design D+ (high school faculty, regular catalog courses, taught on the high school campus). Until recently, most of these options have been available only to able high school seniors.

Many people contend that low- and moderate-achieving students should not have access to concurrent enrollment programs. Economists cite trends that point to increased employment possibilities for janitors, secretaries, store clerks, and other low-status service-sector jobs. They contend that encouraging low- and moderate-achieving students to continue on in college is not in the nation's economic interest, because such individuals could fill these unattractive, yet economically important, service-sector jobs.

Table 1. **Four General Models of School-College Curriculum Articulation Arrangements**

Teaching Responsibility	Course Design			
	Special Design		*Regular Catalog*	
College Faculty	A+	A*	B+	B*
High School Faculty	C+	C*	D+	D*

+ Course taught on high school campus.
* Course taught on college campus.

Source: Adapted from Wilbur and Chapman, 1978.

The counterargument is that limiting opportunity is inconsistent with the mission of public secondary and higher education. Viewed in the context of the historical underrepresentation of women and minorities in leadership roles in industry, education, and government, encouraging the continuation of such a caste system is difficult to justify.

Despite dropout rates of close to 50 percent occurring in many cities, some authorities fear the negative motivational consequences of allowing moderate- and low-achieving high school students to take college courses. According to this view, students are seen as "cruising through high school, being handed every opportunity on a silver platter." Proponents claim that permitting low and moderate achievers to start their college educations in high school, is countermotivational. Although for some critics this argument has an intuitive appeal, there is no empirical data to support this claim. History is full of similar arguments against enhancing opportunities for upward mobility.

The flood gate principle is based on the belief that if any population is given entitlement to rights and privileges, then all must be afforded the same opportunity. This principle has some merit, but the underlying assumption—that such expansion of social and economic opportunity is problematic—is flawed.

Florida, Minnesota, New York, and Oklahoma have already adopted various concurrent enrollment models. (For an overview of state-level initiatives of concurrent enrollment, see American Association for Higher Education . . . , 1986; Aronson and Carlson, 1986; Berman, 1985; "College Option: . . . ," 1985; Seminole County School Board . . . , 1986; Hendrickson, 1986; Maguire, 1986; Minnesota . . . , 1985; Randall, 1986; "State Capitals: . . . ," 1986; Wehrwein, 1986.) Each state has its own model and varying criteria for student selection. These criteria range from open access to all students on demand, to more restrictive requirements negotiated between local school boards and colleges. None of the criteria have been challenged in the courts as inappropriate or in violation of individual rights.

The traditional justification for excluding low- and moderate-achieving students from college-level study in high school is that these students are not bright, skilled, and motivated enough to cope with the demands of college course work. While the subsequent collegiate success after high school graduation by many low- and moderate-achieving students would seem to question the validity of this retort, very few programs that offer the opportunity for college-level study are open to these students. Still fewer programs have been assessed in an empirically rigorous fashion.

Where public institutions are concerned, the funding of concurrent programs poses a final and serious legislative dilemma. Nearly all tax levy funding for both secondary and higher education are predicated on some version of a head count formula. The problem for legislatures and taxing/funding authorities is that in cases where students take classes for simultaneous high school and college credits, both college and high school may claim the student, opening the possibility for double funding claims.

When concurrent enrollment programs service only a few very bright students, for example, local and state authorities can advance ad hoc solutions that do not involve setting precedents or require much money. Broadening the audience to include low and moderate achievers, however, coupled with the possibility of double funding, may lead to problems on an entirely different scale.

A wide variety of solutions to these problems exists for programs in different states. Minnesota allows students to choose between applying their earned course credits to high school or to college graduation requirements—but not to both. On an experimental basis, New York has adopted several models for funding concurrent enrollment; such models simply double-fund the students. Florida has developed a complicated system that allows monies to follow students, while simultaneously reimbursing local school districts for students claimed by community colleges.

Denying Access Has Its Cost

The cost to individuals or to society of excluding low- and moderate-achieving high school students from concurrent college-level study is real. Measured in terms of dollars, the economic and social loss of diminished incentive, or talents and abilities never fully developed for the public good, is significant.

First, what are the lost opportunity costs when society limits access by such students to college study in high school? Consider the loss of human potential. If students capable of college-level work are denied entry to college, that denial limits their development and economic contributions for a lifetime. Academic performance and curriculum tracking are closely associated with race and income, and the challenge to complete Boyer's (1983) unfinished agenda of access and equity is great. (For a discussion of the interrelationship between race and income see Sexton, 1961, p. 177; Higher Education Research Institute, 1982, pp. 47-48; Ramist, 1984, pp. 182-183.) Minority advancement is still a grave concern. Between 1980 and 1984, black enrollment in colleges declined at a time when enrollment for all other groups rose (Rothman, 1986). In this context, the significance of joint enrollment programs for low- and moderate-achieving students emerges. Such programs represent not only an opportunity to earn college credit, but also symbolize society's commitment to equity of opportunity and access.

Second, low to moderate achievers are not given the head start that the highest-achieving students are offered with the opportunity to earn college credit. Programs such as advanced placement give the most able students a significant advantage at the beginning of their college careers. Lower-achieving students, who have a slower and perhaps more tortuous route through higher education, must start at the beginning of the sequence.

Third, low and moderate achievers, often economically disadvantaged, are denied the opportunity to save on tuition costs. With college tuition rising annually, the chance to take college courses in high school, usually at no or greatly reduced expense, is a boon. For middle-income families, often ineligible for anything but limited financial aid, this cost savings can take on added meaning.

A fourth consideration is the potential savings with the reduction of course overlap in colleges and high schools. High school–college curriculum redundancy has been reported frequently and could be alleviated. The joint enrollment model permits students to take courses for simultaneous high school and college credit; yet, historically, it is available only to a small group of the most elite students.

The real dollar cost that results from curriculum redundancy is profound. Osborn (1928) and Blanchard (1971) have both commented on the overlapping nature of the last two years of high school and the first two years of college, all of which is being paid for either in the form of tax levy education aid or college tuition. Blanchard (1971, p. 38) estimated that based on costs and enrollment in 1965, $420 million has been lost. When adjusted by the Bureau of Labor Statistics Consumer Price Index (328.4) alone, and ignoring the much faster rising college costs, this figure represented $1.419 billion in 1986 dollars (U.S. Bureau of the Census, 1986, p. 477).

Any possible costs attributed to denying access to college-level study by low- and moderate-achieving high school seniors are, however, speculative as they are based on the premise that such students can succeed when the opportunity to take college courses is offered.

Examining Three Programs

To determine the extent to which these students can benefit from exposure to college-level study in high school, three high school programs located in New York City were studied during 1985–86. Each program purported to (a) address the needs of low- and moderate-achieving students, and (b) provide the students with opportunities to succeed in college courses while still high school seniors.

Although they shared common characteristics, significant differences in the high school–college collaborative programs facilitated a comparison study of three substantially different archetypal approaches to the high school–college connection.

City-As-School (CAS) is a New York City public alternative high school. Its students select and attend regularly scheduled college courses at various colleges. They are taught by college faculty and sit side-by-side with college students. The program, notwithstanding its alternative school nature, is typical of many programs across the country where educators broker places in local colleges on a space available basis for high school students who earn high school and college credit.

The College Now program is sponsored jointly by the City University of New York and the New York City Board of Education. The program allows students at several public high schools to take preselected Kingsborough Community College courses that are taught on high school campuses by high school teachers operating in the capacity of adjunct college instructors. College Now is typical of a class of articulated programs that attempts to bring college study to high school classrooms.

Middle College High School, located on the campus of City University of New York's LaGuardia Community College, is also an alternative high school. It takes advantage of the intimate curricular liaisons that may be fostered when high schools and colleges coexist on the same campus. Unlike most early college models that exploit this relationship for the benefit of gifted students, the Middle College approach to simultaneous enrollment claims a far different clientele: high-risk students considered potential dropouts. Middle College has easy access to the college campus, shares curricular goals and resources with the host college, and offers intense individualized support for the high school students who enroll in regular college courses at LaGuardia College.

City-As-School. City-As-School's brokerage approach to dual enrollment—placing students in local college classrooms as space is available—is used in many areas. As matters of state educational policy, Minnesota and Oklahoma have adopted different versions of this design (model B* in Table 1).

City-As-School was founded in 1972 as part of the New York City public school system. The primary objective is to link students with hundreds of off-site learning experiences by utilizing community resources. The school was developed as an alternative to classroom-based instruction for disaffected, alienated, and failing high school students from traditional high schools. According to its admission information, "City-As-School accepts a cross-section of the high school population of New York City's five boroughs. They transfer to CAS from regular high schools. Preference is given to students who have completed the ninth and tenth grades and particularly those who have fulfilled two years of mathematics and science" (*City-As-School High School,* 1986a).

City-As-School utilizes colleges located in New York City, registering CAS students for regular college courses (tuition-free) after consulting with a resources coordinator, a CAS teacher who is the liaison with the colleges. Students who pass the college courses receive both college and high school credit for their effort.

CAS claims that 24 percent of their students enroll in college classes; that a profile of a recent graduating class revealed 52 percent of the graduates had attended one or more colleges; and that the passing rate in college classes taken by CAS students was 72 percent (*City-As-School High School*, 1986b).

College Now. Kingsborough Community College's College Now program uses local high school teachers as adjunct college staff to teach regular college courses on high school campuses. It is a model used historically and successfully with high-performing students. One notable example of this program type is Syracuse University's Project Advance. The State of Florida has recently mandated the community colleges to develop similar relationships with local schools.

College Now, begun in fall 1984, works with eight New York City public high schools. Kingsborough selects faculty from each of the high schools to teach preselected college courses on the high school campuses. Students acquire high school and college credit upon satisfactory course completion. In addition to these courses, other remedial courses are offered in writing and math but without the promise of college credit. The program seeks students who are not high performers, hoping to reach moderate achievers, or those students who have between 65 percent and 80 percent cumulative high school averages.

College Now students are offered courses tuition-free. All students must take a battery of CUNY-designed tests (known as the Freshman Assessment Test), which indicate levels of math, reading, and writing competency. Those scoring above the CUNY-prescribed mark are admitted to credit-bearing courses after meeting with visiting college counselors.

Middle College High School. Middle College High School is the latest evolutionary development in a line of programs that traces its origins back to Johns Hopkins University's Three-Year Collegiate Program established in 1876. In addition to the curricular continuity, Middle College provides emotional and developmental support to younger learners with high dropout potential.

To be eligible for admission to Middle College, students must have graduated from a local junior high school and meet the following criteria: "(1) a high rate of absenteeism or (2) three or more subject area failures or (3) identified social and emotional problems stemming from the home environment or (4) evidence of some potential, which [Middle College faculty] interprets as present in all students" (Lieberman, 1986, p. 3).

According to Board of Education figures in 1979, approximately 53 percent of Middle College students were more than two years retarded in reading, and 40 percent were more than two years retarded in math. During the 1985–86 school year, the ethnic distribution of the student body was 45 percent white, 33 percent Hispanic, 21 percent black, and 1 percent Asian, with about 40 percent of the 486 students on public assistance (Lieberman, 1986, pp. 4-5).

In addition to a comprehensive cooperative education program, which mirrors that of LaGuardia College, Middle College students can take courses at the college for simultaneous high school and college credit. Middle College counselors interview students who desire to take college classes to determine eligibility. That same counselor will monitor the student's progress periodically during the college experience.

Lieberman (1986) reports that ninety Middle College students take college courses each year, with a range of one to fifteen credits earned. She also reports that in over eleven years, 500 students or 30 percent of the Middle College students have taken and completed college courses (p. 13).

Students as Low and Moderate Achievers

Based on a comparison of six variables (overall high school average, high school rank in class, California Achievement Tests in Reading and in Math, and Scholastic Aptitude Tests—Verbal and Math), it was concluded that each of three programs in the study served moderate and low achievers. Figures 1-4 provide summary comparisons of local samples with national data sources.

City-As-School. Overall as a group, City-As-School students appeared to rank below national groups in four of the six indicators of performance and ability.

College Now. College Now students had a significantly lower mean cumulative high school average, and the distribution for this variable differed significantly from the national sample, with more averages in the lower ranges. Overall, College Now students were significantly different and lower in five of six variables. Based on this evidence, College Now students could be classified as low and moderate achievers.

Middle College. Middle College students' mean high school average and percentile rank were lower than the national samples, and the local distributions for the two variables differed significantly from the national populations. Yet, the high school average had greater concentrations of high range averages than the national sample, while no conclusions could be drawn about differences in class rank.

Standardized test scores, however, presented an unmistakable pattern. Middle College students consistently had significantly lower means, along with scores distributed at the lowest-value ranges of the national samples. This conclusion held true for both CATs and SATs. Based on four of six available measures, Middle College was clearly a school of low- and moderate-ability students.

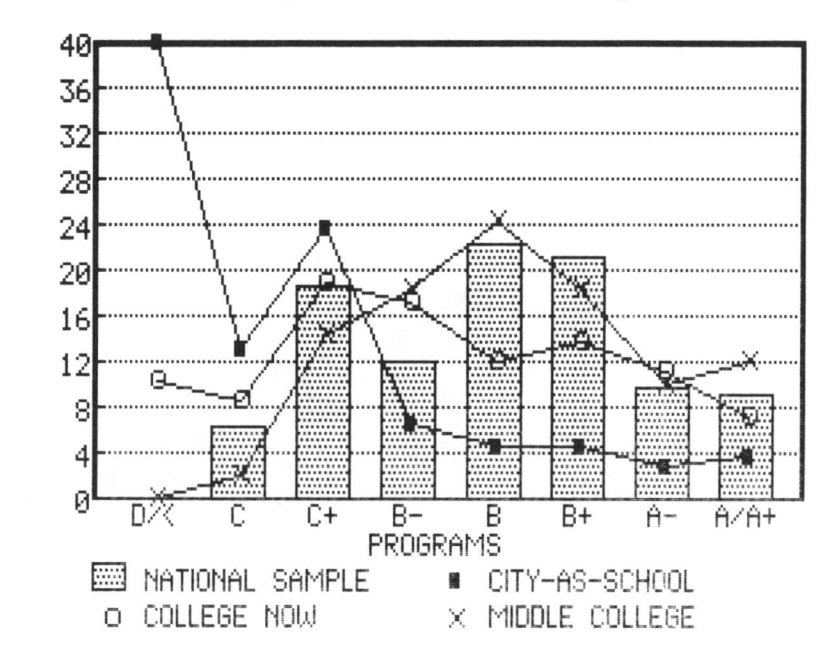

Figure 1. High School Grade Point Average

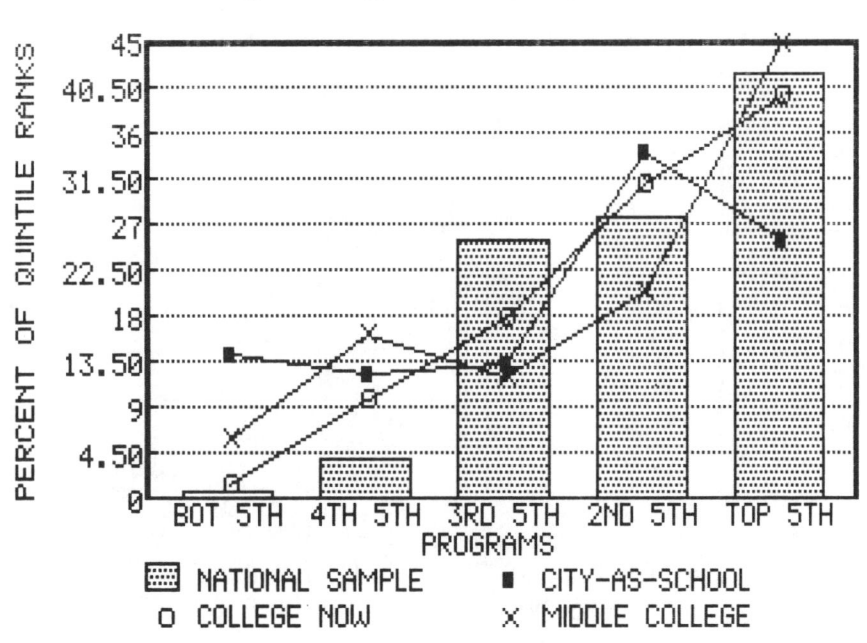

□ NATIONAL SAMPLE   ■ CITY-AS-SCHOOL
○ COLLEGE NOW   × MIDDLE COLLEGE

Figure 2. High School Rank in Class

□ NATIONAL SAMPLE   ■ CITY-AS-SCHOOL
○ COLLEGE NOW   × MIDDLE COLLEGE

Figure 3. Scholastic Aptitude Test (Verbal) Scores

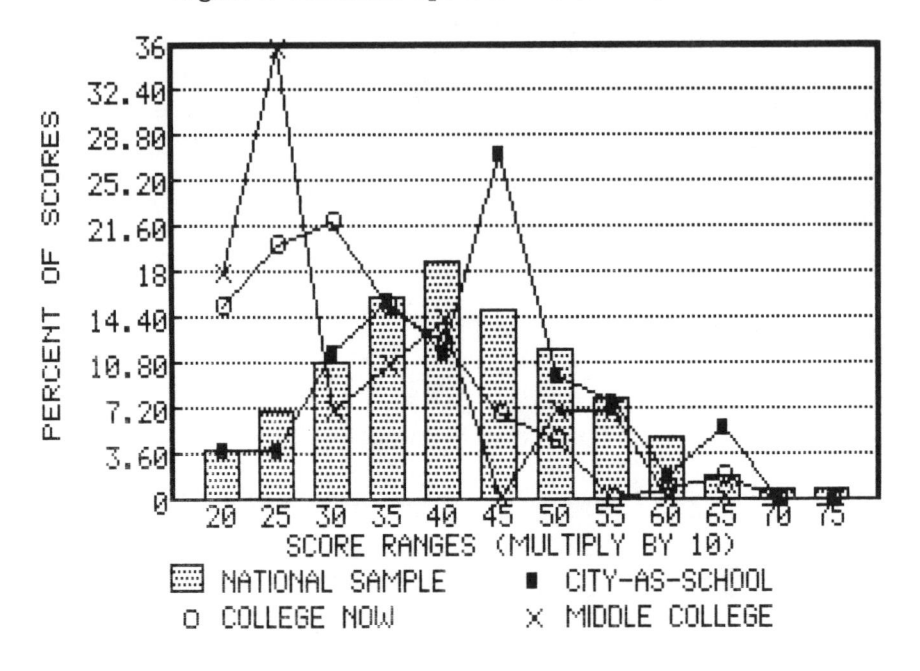

Figure 4. Scholastic Aptitude Test (Math) Scores

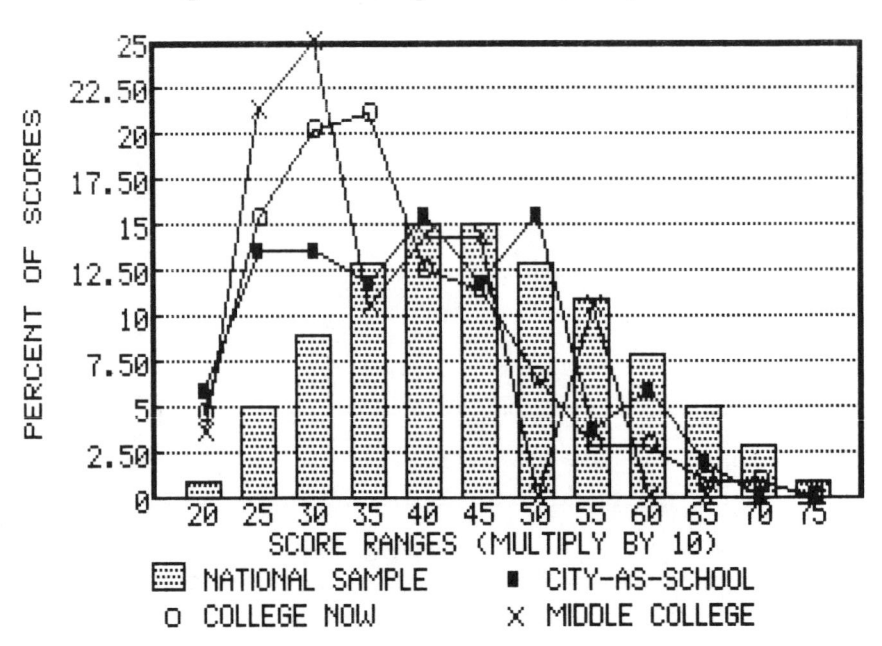

Program Students and GPA in College Courses

The measure of success used in this analysis was the college grade point average (GPA). Using the national freshman sample maintained by the Cooperative Institutional Research Program (CIRP) at University of California, Los Angeles, students in the local study were compared to the larger sample of 20,000.

City-As-School students earned the lowest GPA, slightly above a C average. College Now students earned the highest GPA, slightly below a B minus average. Middle College students earned a GPA of nearly C+. GPA distributions for each of the programs also differed significantly from the national freshman class. City-As-School and Middle College had concentrations of grades in the lower-grade values. College Now had an uneven distribution that contrasted with the national sample. As a result, College Now's distribution was evaluated as equivalent, although clearly not identical, to the national freshman sample. Figures 5, 6, and 7 illustrate the comparisons between the three programs studied and the national sample of college freshmen.

Students in each program earned slightly better than two-thirds of the college credits they registered for.

Given the prior assessment that all three programs comprised low and moderate achievers, the college results seem appropriate. College Now did the best. Despite their poor skills, Middle College students persevered, earning two-thirds of the credits for which they registered and maintaining an overall average of nearly C+. Although they had the best skills of any group tested, City-As-College students struggled the most but maintained a C average, and at the same time passed two-thirds of the credits for which they registered.

Variables Correlated with College Grade Point Average

High school average was the only variable that was a significant correlate of college course grade point average in all three programs. Table 2 shows the various correlates of college GPA for each of the programs studied. Correlation coefficients indicate that a variable was significantly correlated with college GPA for a particular program.

The following information summarizes the findings from the programs studied:

1. All three programs served low and moderate achievers, with each program serving greater proportions of low and moderate achievers than the national samples. However, each program varied from the others in the strength of its difference with the national samples.

2. Students in each of the three programs earned approximately two-thirds of the college credits for which they registered.

Figure 5. College Course Grade Point Average, National Sample and City-As-School

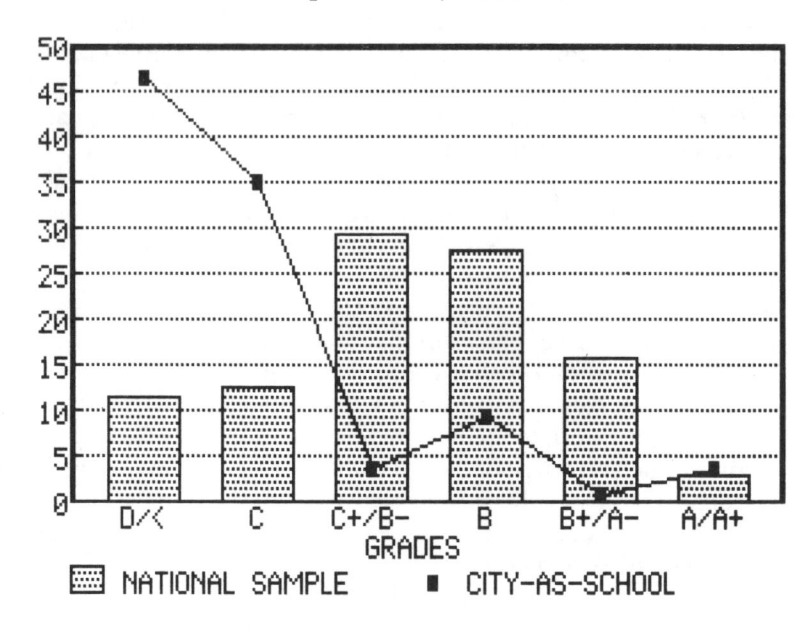

Figure 6. College Course Grade Point Average, National Sample and College Now

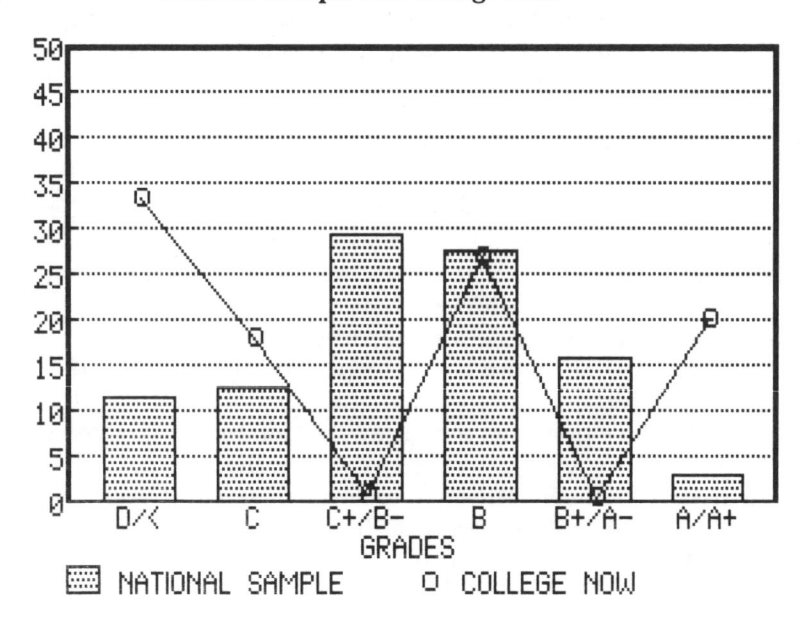

Figure 7. College Course Grade Point Average, National Sample and Middle College

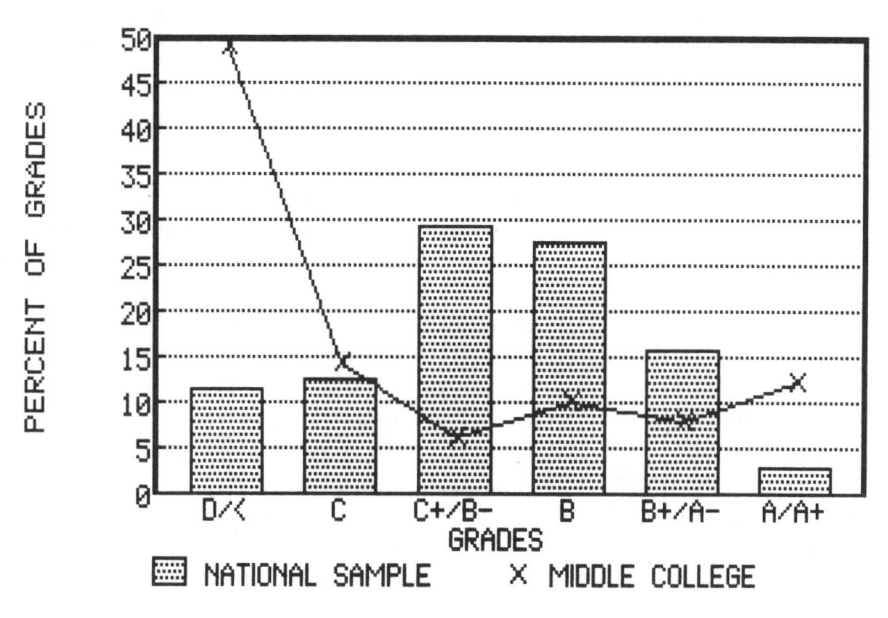

3. Students in each of the programs earned college GPAs that differed significantly from a national sample of first-year college students.

4. City-As-School and Middle College students earned greater proportions of low college grades than did students in the national sample of first-year college students. College Now students seemed to more closely approximate college freshman performance.

5. High school average correlated with GPA in college courses in all three programs. Rank in class was associated with GPA in College Now and Middle College. The CAT-R was correlated in City-As-School (negatively) and College Now (positively). The SAT-M, SAT-V, and CAT-M

Table 2. Correlates of College Grade Point Average

Correlates	City-As-School	College Now	Middle College
High School Average	.2667	.4041	.4538
CAT-R	−.3054	.2773	
Class Rank		.2660	.4348
SAT-M		.4200	
SAT-V		.3384	
CAT-M		.3114	
Gender			.4157

were uniquely associated with GPA in College Now, while gender was correlated in Middle College.

If, as it appears from the programs studied, low- and moderate-achieving high school students can be accelerated into college study, implications for policymakers must be explored.

Recommendations

Many of the leaders in the contemporary education reform movement, but Ernest Boyer foremost among them, have discussed the need to reevaluate the fundamental curricular and structural assumptions of the transition from high school to college. The findings that many low and moderate achievers can perform relatively well in college-level courses while still in high school underscores the need to take a fresh look at articulation practices. Clearly, the findings indicate that a much broader range of students than previously acknowledged as appropriate can succeed when offered the opportunity to pursue college coursework in high school.

In the three programs studied, the only factor consistently associated with college course GPA was high school average. Controlling this variable, however, can significantly shape the profile of grade point averages in college courses. Table 3 shows that raising the minimum entry-level high school average for each of the programs studied affects the percentage of grades of D or less.

The purpose of this sensitivity analysis is to illustrate that restricting college courses exclusively to the elite class of students with averages of 90 percent and above is unnecessary.

Clearly, not everyone is capable of taking advantage of early college study. On the other hand, the research can persuade educators and policymakers to transcend the obvious when looking for factors that may be associated with success. If one is willing to accept a slightly greater risk of failure, a somewhat lower academic entry standard, perhaps in combi-

Table 3. Effect of High School Average on Grades of D or Less

High School Averages Included	*Percent Grades D or Less*		
	City-As-School	College Now	Middle College
All	46.7	33.5	49.0
> 70	38.1	31.8	49.0
> 73	30.6	30.2	47.9
> 77	25.0	29.4	41.5
> 80	17.6	26.1	31.3

nation with greater student support, the result might be more than acceptable. One idea is very clear, however. One need not be brilliant to take and pass a college class while in high school.

Why then do educators insist that only the gifted students are capable of college-level study in high school? The answer is tied to economic issues. The causal factors can actually be found in the history of high school–college relations and the abyss that has historically existed between colleges and secondary schools.

The research here suggests the potential that can be realized by permitting motivated low and moderate achievers to engage in college study in high school. As the three programs in the study suggest, we must continue to investigate the correlates of success in college-level study and shape the design of programs based on the impact of the variables identified.

The responsibility to anticipate and provide support for varying levels of student need is a shared one. If high schools and colleges are going to continue to offer low and moderate achievers the opportunity to take college courses for simultaneous high school and college credit, then those institutions must provide the support structures necessary to enhance the possibilities of student success.

Clearly, relationships exist between instructional delivery systems, student need profiles, student support services, and student success in college-level work. Even if success cannot be guaranteed, its probability can be enhanced through careful program management.

When one considers the possible benefits to individual low- and moderate-achieving students—traditionally bypassed by opportunity—and the potential gains to society that might result from encouraging the success of such students, moving away from the traditional, limited view of their capabilities is more than justified.

References

American Association for Higher Education, National Association of Secondary School Principals and Syracuse University Project Advance. *National Survey of School-College Partnerships.* Syracuse, N.Y.: Syracuse University, 1986.

Aronson, R., and Carlson, R. *Open Enrollment and Postsecondary Options: Lessons from the Minnesota Experience* (Cassette Recording No. 430 8688). Reston, Va.: National Association of Secondary School Principals, Feb. 1986.

Berman, P. "The Next Step: The Minnesota Plan." *Phi Delta Kappan,* 1985, *67* (3), 188–193.

Blanchard, B. E. *A National Survey of Curriculum Articulation Between the College of Liberal Arts and the Secondary School.* Chicago: De Paul University, 1971.

Boyer, E. L. *High School: A Report on Secondary Education in America.* New York: Harper & Row, 1983.

Boyer, E. L. *College: The Undergraduate Experience Education in America.* New York: Harper & Row, 1987.

City-As-School High School. "Admission Information." New York: City-As-School High School, 1986a.
City-As-School High School. "College Studies." New York: City-As-School High School, 1986b.
"College Option: Best of Both Worlds." *New York Times,* Oct. 29, 1985, pp. Cl, C6.
Hendrickson, A. D. "Backtalk: Readers Oppose the Minnesota Plan." *Phi Delta Kappan,* 1986, *67* (9), 695.
Higher Education Research Institute. *The American Freshman: National Norms for Fall 1982.* Los Angeles: American Council on Education, University of California, 1982.
Kleinrock, K. J. *Concurrent Enrollment Programs: A Summative Description and Proposals for Student Services.* Unpublished doctoral dissertation, Teachers College, Columbia University, 1986.
Lieberman, J. *Ford Foundation Proposal.* Long Island City, N.Y.: LaGuardia Community College, 1986.
Maguire, N. D. "Backtalk: Readers Oppose the Minnesota Plan." *Phi Delta Kappan,* 1986, *67* (9), 695.
Minnesota 1985 Omnibus School Aids Act, Article 5, Section 1, Subdivision 4, Aug. 2, 1985, p. 10.
Osborn, J. W. *Overlapping and Omission in Our Course of Study.* Bloomington, Ill.: Public School Publishing Company, 1928.
Ramist, L. "Predictive Validity of the ATP Tests." In T. F. Donlon (ed.), *The College Board Technical Handbook for the Scholastic Aptitude Test and Achievement Tests.* New York: College Entrance Examination Board, 1984.
Randall, R. "Options Are Changing the Face of Education in Minnesota." *School Administrator,* 1986, *43* (5), 14–16.
Rothman, R. "Enrollment Gains Linked to Marketing." *Education Week,* Oct. 15, 1986, p. 8.
Seminole County School Board and Seminole Community College. "1983 Florida Administrative Code, Rule 61-10.241." In *Agreement for the Admission of Students for Accelerated Programs (Dual Enrollments).* Sanford, Fla.: Seminole County School Board and Seminole Community College, 1986.
Sexton, P. C. *Education and Income.* New York: Viking Penguin, 1961.
"State Capitals: Minnesota—School Aid Cut Less Than One Percent." *Education Week,* Apr. 16, 1986, p. 8.
U.S. Bureau of the Census. *Statistical Abstract of the United States, 1986.* Prepared by Department of Commerce, Bureau of the Census. Washington, D.C., 1986.
Wehrwein, A. C. "Perpich Drops Open Enrollment Plan." *Education Week,* May 28, 1986, p. 6.
Wilbur, F. P., and Chapman, D. W. *College Courses in the High School.* Reston: Va.: National Association of Secondary School Principals, 1978.

Arthur Richard Greenberg is dean of freshman skills and associate dean of faculty at LaGuardia Community College, City University of New York. He has also served as principal of Beach Channel High School in Rockaway Park, New York, and of Middle College of LaGuardia Community College.

Hard work, commitment, and cooperation among three educational entities have created a dual enrollment program that will encompass grades ten through the master's degree.

New World School of the Arts: Beyond Dual Enrollment

Katharine Muller

Dual enrollment and other cooperative arrangements between public school systems and local community colleges are not new. Programs emphasizing performing and visual arts have been in existence for many years. What *is* new is a cooperative venture between a public school system and a community college that grew to include a state university and to become an entity in its own right—the New World School of the Arts in Miami, Florida.

In 1975 the Dade County Public Schools (DCPS) wanted to more fully integrate by attracting white and Hispanic students to those schools essentially all black. One idea quickly gained support: placing specialized programs for gifted students in predominantly black schools. These magnet programs took many different forms, but one proposed by visual arts teacher Marcy Sarmiento expanded beyond anyone's wildest dreams. Sarmiento developed a Performing and Visual Arts Center (later known as PAVAC) at essentially all-black Northwestern Senior High. Two years later—after the school theater had been refurbished and dance, music, and choral studios built—the center became a reality, offering specialized training in the arts during the last three class periods of the day and an

J. E. Lieberman (ed.). *Collaborating with High Schools.*
New Directions for Community Colleges, no. 63. San Francisco: Jossey-Bass, Fall 1988.

extended period after school. The program attracted students interested in either the full day or in only afternoon classes, enhancing integration of the school in a positive way.

About the same time, Miami-Dade Community College (MDCC) began a comprehensive Emphasis on Excellence program that included an honors program. A few years later, a summer program for gifted junior high students and the governor's summer program for gifted high school students were added. While planning the two summer gifted programs, Kandell Bentley-Baker, coordinator of the Emphasis on Excellence program at the North Campus of MDCC, visited the PAVAC program at Northwestern. Excited by what she found, Bentley-Baker collaborated with Sarmiento and obtained the agreement of Dade County Public Schools and Miami-Dade Community College to expand the summer program to include talented as well as gifted students. Sarmiento also wanted to expand the PAVAC concept to other Dade County high schools, but providing adequate facilities was a major obstacle. Enrollment patterns at the college offered a solution. Students at the college tended to enroll mornings or evenings, leaving the excellent performing and visual arts facilities on campus relatively dormant in the afternoon.

Serendipitously, the Florida Legislature enacted legislation in the spring of 1980 to promote cooperation between secondary schools and state colleges and universities by establishing dual enrollment policies. Recognizing possible benefits for both the school system and the college, Sarmiento and Bentley-Baker drafted a proposal for a cooperative dual enrollment approach to PAVAC. The proposal received support from administrators in both systems.

A Pilot Program Proves Successful

In the summer of 1981, a pilot dual enrollment PAVAC program began drawing students from sixteen of the twenty-four county high schools. The show of interest convinced school and college officials to establish PAVAC programs in the fall of 1982 at both the north and south campuses of the college, thus making the program accessible to students from all over the county. The programs drew students from all twenty-four high schools. Margaret Pelton and Richard Janaro coordinated the program at the MDCC South Campus, while Bentley-Baker coordinated the program at the MDCC North Campus, and Sarmiento became the DCPS coordinator.

Designing a Dual Enrollment Arts Program

Curriculum Development. School and college faculty jointly developed the PAVAC curriculum. Much planning was required to develop a curriculum that met course content and graduation requirements for both institutions. In addition, any courses that were new to the college or had been offered in a different credit configuration had to be submitted to the Office of the State Course Numbering System for approval. No special designation was placed on either the high school or college transcript to indicate a dual enrollment course.

Auditions. To be accepted into the PAVAC program students had to audition or present a portfolio. A panel made up of MDCC faculty, DCPS faculty, and community artists judged the students to determine who should enter the program. In addition to showing talent, students must have maintained a C average in all high school or junior high coursework for the year prior to acceptance into PAVAC. The college waived for PAVAC students the standard assessment test given to all entering students. To remain in the program, PAVAC students were required to maintain a C average in all academic courses and a B average in all arts courses. Musical theater, theater, and music majors were also required to perform for a jury twice a semester, and faculty wrote progress evaluations on all students at the end of each year.

Faculty. Faculty for the PAVAC classes were drawn from the public schools, the college, and the community. If neither school system had a full-time faculty member who was highly qualified, then an adjunct professor was hired. Miami-Dade faculty who taught in the program could have PAVAC classes as part of their regular load or as an overload, depending upon departmental assignments. Dade County Public School teachers were assigned full time to the PAVAC program. All adjunct professors were paid by Miami-Dade, while DCPS paid for occasional contractual services, such as a costumer, set designer, or choreographer.

Additional monies were available to bring in outstanding performers and teachers to conduct master classes and workshops. Such luminaries as acting teacher Uta Hagen, dancers Edward Villella and Allegra Kent, sculptor Duane Hanson, and director Joshua Logan conducted master classes for the PAVAC students. These opportunities would not have been available to students scattered in high schools throughout the county, nor would the different and well-equipped art studios, ballet classes, and private voice and instrument lessons have been affordable for many students and their families. The students paid no money for the intensive instruction.

Arts Programs. PAVAC encompassed five areas of study: dance, theater, musical theater, music (both voice and instrument), and visual arts. In some instances, students took classes in more than one area. From the beginning, the program placed heavy demands on students. After they attended their regular high school in the morning for five periods of academic subjects, they were bussed after lunch to the college where they took performing and visual arts classes for three periods, extending the school day two periods beyond that of their peers.

Credits. Students in the PAVAC program attended a minimum of three hours of art classes each afternoon at the college. For these classes they earned two high school elective credits and twelve college credits for the school year. A normal high school schedule was six periods with an elective seventh period. PAVAC students attended the equivalent of eight periods. Attendance in the eighth period class was mandatory, and although no separate credit was given for the class, coursework was graded and averaged into the grades of the other two art classes. Program directors found that high school students needed more hours on task to accomplish the equivalent of college credits. To earn the same twelve credits college students could earn during fall and winter terms, PAVAC students attended classes fall, winter, and spring terms. Following the normal high school schedule, PAVAC students attended class five days a week. A college student would attend the same class three days a week for fewer weeks.

Potentially, a student who had been in PAVAC for three years (grades ten through twelve) could enter Miami-Dade with thirty-six college credits of arts electives. In reality, once at the college level, students generally wanted to continue with advanced arts classes, so they often earned more credits than required for an associate in arts degree. Thus, PAVAC students often entered college at the sophomore or junior level in arts. No general education required courses were part of those earned in PAVAC.

Cost. The high school courses, including studio and individualized music instruction, were free to the students. Dual enrollment college credit was given at no extra cost. However, students who continued in the arts programs at MDCC after high school graduation paid regular MDCC tuition unless they received a scholarship or other financial aid. To aid PAVAC graduates and other arts students, MDCC created 100 arts scholarships which covered the costs of tuition, private lessons, and a $50 materials allowance for studio courses.

Funding. State funding formulas for dual enrollment programs changed almost on an yearly basis. Both MDCC and DCPS wanted PAVAC to succeed, emphasizing budgets to support the program. The college contributed facilities, coordinators, and support staff, MDCC faculty salaries for PAVAC classes taught, and a departmental budget. Dade County Public Schools provided a coordinator, faculty, and a departmental budget. Departmental budgets paid for books, art supplies, transportation, adjunct instructors, contractual services, and miscellaneous expenses.

Schedule. Originally, the program was designed so that students spent Monday through Thursday in studio classes; Fridays were reserved for special classes such as art appreciation, choreography, or portfolio. This flexibility in the schedule proved to be unworkable as program directors discovered the students needed more structure. Scheduling was subsequently rearranged so that all classes met five days a week, and special activities were accommodated where appropriate in the schedule.

The school calendar for PAVAC students followed that of the public schools, not that of the college. Therefore, the teachers most affected were college faculty who sometimes found themselves teaching PAVAC classes when the college was on break and other times teaching their regular classes when PAVAC classes were not in session.

Philosophical Issues

A philosophical issue that absorbed the faculty and administrators of the school system and the college was the amount of public exposure the students should be given. In the early years of the program, public student performances were frequent because program directors felt more visibility would increase support and funding for the program. Once PAVAC was established, public performances were cut back. Clearly performance is part of the training in any arts program, but the underlying philosophy of the program was that pushing performance over training was detrimental to the students' development and contributed to an inflated sense of their talents for students who already knew they were special. Program directors strove to create a balance between the intense competition, which naturally occurs among a highly talented group of students helping to create individual success, and the recognition that the extended day and intensive training alone placed extra burdens on the students.

Student Success. Dreams of glory and the accolades that awaited them fired students' imagination as they worked hard to achieve greater skill. Some of those dreams were not unfounded. In the first few years, students graduating from the PAVAC program won awards from the National Foundation for Advancement of the Arts and scholarships to continue studies at such places as Pratt Institute, NYU, CAL-Arts, Eastman School of Music, North Carolina School of the Arts, Parsons Institute, American Ballet Theater II, Sarah Lawrence, and Howard University. In recent years, as many as 75 percent of the graduates of the program received scholarship offers.

Administrative Support. Support from top-level administrators was both strong and crucial. Sympathetic administrators with the vision to see the potential for the program were essential. The college took the lead in lobbying the legislature for additional funds, while the school system established arts magnet centers in elementary and junior high schools to provide a feeder system for PAVAC. In addition, the college began an arts scholarship program that allowed PAVAC graduates to continue their studies at MDCC. To be fair, not all arts teachers supported the program; some felt it drew the most talented students from their own classes—an allegation that had some validity. However, PAVAC eliminated much of that response by recruiting students at the end of the ninth grade before they entered high school.

Expanding the Concept

By the fall of 1983, some 240 students were enrolled in the PAVAC program with many more preparing to audition for the next year. The community began to take notice of the program, and administrators felt it was a success. The college went to the legislature asking that PAVAC be designated a Center for Excellence, a designation created by the legislature to support community college regional programs of specialized training for which additional funding is allocated. The designation was not awarded; instead, at the insistence of a powerful local legislator, Florida International University (FIU) was added to the cooperative arrangement, and $50,000 was allocated to plan a South Florida School of the Arts (later renamed New World School of the Arts) as a high school and college for the performing and visual arts. The PAVAC program had the potential of becoming a school that would offer high school through master's degree in the fine arts.

Planning. A project director was hired and with a steering committee of thirty-five representing the arts, business, and education began planning for the new school in the fall of 1984. Five national consultants connected with well-established arts schools were brought to conduct a community symposium, work with the committee, and make recommendations. The committee then prepared a comprehensive report on philosophy, curriculum, faculty selection, student selection, governance, community relations, and facilities that was submitted to the legislature in the spring of 1985. The legislature responded with a $200,000 grant to continue planning.

Curriculum Development. The Performing and Visual Arts Center continued as a full program with PAVAC faculty joining with faculty of DCPS, MDCC, FIU, and University of Miami (included because FIU lacked a film and video program) to create the first drafts of program curricula for the new school. A total of fifty-five faculty members worked months to develop curricula that met high school graduation requirements and the requirements of MDCC and FIU, as well as matched the state course numbering system. Trying to meet the needs of students and three disparate institutional entities was not an easy task, but the commitment and dedication of faculty and administrators overcame the difficulties. Everyone believed in this vision that offered an opportunity to build a truly unique institution. Funding from the legislature continued with a $500,000 grant in the spring of 1986 and was boosted by a $500,000 endowment for a scholarship competition for Florida students from the North Carolina National Bank. The $500,000 legislative grant was earmarked to hire a provost and other staff personnel and to begin facilities preparation and equipment purchase.

Provost Named. That summer, a search committee reviewed 175 applications for the position of provost and in the fall of 1986 selected Richard Klein, principal of LaGuardia High School for Music and the Arts in New York City. He immediately began working with community leaders, faculty, and administrators of the three sponsoring institutions to prepare for the opening of the New World School of the Arts (NWSA). The public schools appointed Alan Weiss principal of NWSA high school. Klein and Weiss worked with selection committees to hire deans for each of the arts division. The deans hired their own arts faculty, and Weiss hired all high school faculty.

New Location

The steering committee and national consultants had recommended that NWSA be a separate school that students attended all day, a school where both academic and art classes would be taught. This would give students a sense of identification with the school and avoid dividing their school day. A central location close to the MDCC Wolfson Campus in downtown Miami would be ideal. Students would have relatively easy access from locations all over the county, campus facilities could be used for the academic courses, services could be provided that would not then be duplicated in the new facility, and students would be close to the myriad cultural activities taking place downtown. City of Miami officials also have plans for an arts district that will encompass the NWSA location, another reason for choosing the downtown site. An early promotional brochure for the school expressed the excitement and possibilities felt by planners:

> Downtown Miami, in the heart of the proposed arts district, is the site selected for the school. Students will have access to the opera, musical theater, and symphony halls to be developed by county and city governments. In addition, the Knight Center, Gusman Hall, and the Fine Arts Center are only a few blocks away. The multifaceted Bayside Project, to begin construction in 1986, will be across the street transforming downtown's Biscayne Boulevard into a hub of shops, restaurants, art galleries, and entertainment centers. Once completed, Bayside, the school, and other components of the arts district will make downtown Miami one of America's few "walking" cities.
>
> This exciting matrix of business, cultural, and educational centers creates an active, cosmopolitan environment for Greater Miami and an ideal location to bring talented students, professional artists, and audiences together. Metrorail and the downtown people mover will be less than one block from the campus.

New World School of the Arts Opens

In the fall of 1987, the New World School of the Arts became a reality, opening its doors to 405 students in grades ten through twelve. Some students were continuing students from the PAVAC program; others were new to the program. The first year of college will be offered in the new facility in the fall of 1988. To enter the college level all students, even those continuing, must audition and be accepted. Dual enrollment will continue for the NWSA high school. Upon graduation from high school, students will continue their college studies in the same location under the aegis of the NWSA. All classes will be offered by the NWSA, but MDCC will be the institution awarding the associate in arts degree, and FIU will be the institution awarding the bachelor's and master's degrees. Miami-Dade Community College has set aside at least fifty scholarships a year for students in the freshman and sophomore years of the NWSA college level. Financial aid will be available just as it is for any qualified student, and tuition will be the same low cost as for all MDCC students. When students reach the junior, senior, and master's levels, they will pay the same tuition as any FIU student. Students will also follow the school calendar of the major credit-granting institution of the level in which they are enrolled.

Fiscal Responsibility. From the beginning, the college has served as the fiscal agent for the new school. As fiscal agent, the college's board of trustees is required to approve all items and expenditures for the NWSA, just as it does for all college expenditures. The college will continue in this role. Therefore, college policies and procedures must be followed for all purchases, contracts, and hiring of NWSA personnel. For this purpose, during the first year of operation of the NWSA, the legislature made a separate appropriation of $800,000 to the school. Each of the member institutions has contributed additional funds.

Staffing. Of the current staff of the school, the high school principal and twenty-eight high school teachers, including four arts teachers, have been hired by DCPS and are responsible to the DCPS board. All other staff are considered NWSA staff, who are hired by MDCC as the fiscal agent of the school and are subject to MDCC policies and procedures. NWSA staff includes the provost, vice-provost, director of program development, business manager, four teaching deans, one full-time faculty, thirty-one adjunct professors, administrative assistant, and clerical staff. As the school grows to include the upper division college, FIU will increase its contributions to the school.

Many of the original faculty and administrators whose commitment and vision gave birth to the New World School of the Arts joined the staff of the new school. They provided continuity and an understanding of the institutional systems as well as long-term commitment. An exciting group of newcomers became deans of dance (Daniel Lewis from Julliard and director of the José Limon Dance Company), music (John de Lancie, formerly director of the Curtis Institute), and visual art (Ed Love, formerly professor of art at Howard University and a Guggenheim Fellow). A program in film and video will be added to the school in the fall of 1988.

Governance. The cooperative efforts among the three institutions that make up the NWSA have been evident throughout all stages of the development of the school, from planning to curriculum development to governance. A formal governance agreement and a joint facilities use agreement exist among the three sponsoring institutions. The executive board for the school has eighteen members; each sponsoring institution appoints six as follows: two administrators, one board member, and three private citizens. The school is in the process of developing a foundation board whose main function will be to generate more community involvement and private funding for the school.

Now that the vision is a reality and the efforts of so many believers and committed supporters have come to fruition, it remains for the staff of the school to build onto the program so that six years from now the school will be truly complete with a student body ranging from the tenth grade students through master's degree seekers. When fully established, the NWSA expects to draw students from all over the United States and Latin America for the college program. In the words of Robert McCabe, president of Miami-Dade Community College and one of the school's strongest supporters, "The promise is extraordinary. I think we'll look back five to ten years from now and say, 'Boy, wasn't this a great day for Miami'."

Katharine Muller is director of academic programs for the Miami-Dade Community College District Office. She coordinates honors programs, district arts programs, international education, and lifelong learning.

The Virginia Peninsula trains technicians for new-technology jobs in electronics through vocational-technical education.

Enabling Professionalism: The Master Technician Program

Doris K. Wimmer

In a time of rapidly changing technology, a great need exists for systems-oriented technicians who can install, operate, maintain, repair, and analyze problems with complex systems. The need for individuals who are masters of their trade has ultimately led to the development of the Master Technician Program, which trains people for specialized occupations in the fields of electronics and/or electromechanical technology.

Specialists in new technology have an in-depth involvement with complex systems in a world of quickly changing technical content. Performance of new-technology skills requires a broad base of technical knowledge that enables workers to be flexible yet apply basic processes to electronics/electromechanical systems. Functioning in a world of new technology requires special skills for production, testing, installation, and maintenance. In order to perform these functions, the master technician must be competent in electricity, electronics, mechanics, optics, pneumatics, fluids, and thermal applications.

Although the curriculum plan is called a "two-plus-two program," emphasis is placed on a comprehensive, coordinated curriculum that spans two levels of instruction. Students in the program combine their secondary education with two additional years at the community college to earn an Associate in Applied Science (AAS) degree in electronics/electromechanical technology. The AAS degree can be transferred to a four-year university, where a student can then earn a degree in engineering technology.

The program is made possible by and its progress ensured through collaboration with business, industry, and government employers who will hire the students when they complete the program. Skilled master technicians can be employed in such settings as the production areas of industry, the sales/service branches of business, and the research/development laboratories of government and higher education. Business, industry, and government look to vocational-technical education to work with such disciplines as mathematics and science and to provide the interdisciplinary curriculum structure needed to produce a master technician. Vocational-technical preparation at both the secondary and postsecondary levels includes instruction of basic competencies in reading, writing, listening and speaking; specialized skills in mathematics and sciences; technical competencies in areas such as electrical and electronics devices, fluid power devices, optical devices, and microcomputers; and application of basic skills in the use of tools, materials, processes, controls, and energy conversion systems.

The Master Technician Program is a project of the Virginia Peninsula local education agencies in cooperation with business, industry, and government. It is governed by the Virginia Department of Education and the Virginia Community College System.

Project Formation

In 1984, Governor Charles M. Robb of Virginia expressed an interest in linkages between secondary and postsecondary educational institutions. This interest led to a series of meetings between various representatives of the Virginia State Board of Education and the Virginia Community College System Board to develop a project based on the two-plus-two concept.

Based on previous success in several areas, the Virginia Peninsula was chosen as the site to develop and pilot the model program. This location was chosen for three specific reasons. First, the Peninsula educational agencies of Thomas Nelson Community College, the regional New Horizons Technical Center, and the school divisions of Hampton, Newport News, Poquoson, Williamsburg/James City County, and York County had worked together successfully to initiate an earlier articulation process using competency-based vocational education. Second, the Virginia Peninsula Vocational Training Council (VPVTC), a collaboration of regional business, industry, and government education, had been formed to serve as a communication link and to dispense occupational specifications from business and industry to education. The VPVTC published "Forecasts of Occupational Demand," containing statistical information and characteristics of a selected occupation, competencies expected of entry-level employees in the occupation, and additional research data. The "Forecast of Occupational Demand for Electronics/Electromechanical Technology" served as the curriculum base for the entire Master Technician Program. Third, the Virginia Peninsula is known for its many business, industry, and government jobs in high technology. It is estimated that on the Peninsula alone over two hundred job openings will be available this year in electronics-related fields. The U.S. Department of Labor anticipates some 8,000 people will be employed in electronics or electric trades by 1990 in the Tidewater of Virginia. Projections are that jobs will be available at Newport News Shipbuilding, the Peninsula's largest employer, as well as at the National Aeronautics and Space Administration (NASA).

Based on the need to keep up with new technology and the growing local and national need for workers in the electronics field, academic and vocational educators and representatives from business, industry, and government began to plan and develop the Secondary/Postsecondary Program to Prepare Master Technicians. These representatives believed this program should assist students to achieve academic excellence while training them for opportunities that would realistically be available to them. According to the business representatives, students completing the program would be highly trained in both electronics and mechanics. They would learn how to interpret technical materials, draft plans, operate and maintain electronic hardware, and keep scientific records.

Educators' commitment to this project was shown in a written agreement signed by the chief executive officers of each local education agency. Commitment was also demonstrated by business, industry, and government through active participation by management-level officials who were on the collaboration council and technician-level workers who were consultants to the writing team.

The curriculum-writing team included math, science, and vocational education instructors from secondary and postsecondary education. Using the validated competencies from the "Forecasts of Occupational Demand," the writing team developed a curriculum that is a unique blend of academics and vocational education and that allows students to obtain competencies in order to directly begin work or to further their education at the community college and beyond.

An executive committee was formed to set policies and procedures for the operation of the project. This executive committee included the vocational directors from each local school division, the director of the technical center, the community college dean of instruction, a representative of the superintendents, and a business representative of the collaboration council.

Project director Cecil G. Phillips of Thomas Nelson Community College and associate director Robert D'Agostino, a secondary vocational education instructor, assumed overall responsibility for the administration of the three-year project.

Project Innovations

The Master Technician Program is recognized as being innovative in four areas.

Two-Plus-Two. Students can combine secondary education with postsecondary training to obtain an AAS degree in electronics/electromechanical technology. Unlike many articulation agreements, no advanced standing is awarded at the community college. Instead, the curriculum is coordinated at both levels to avoid duplication of competency instruction and to provide a smooth transition from secondary to postsecondary education.

Student Flexibility. The program is designed to allow maximum flexibility in career options. Students may continue their education as far as they wish or go to work at any point. Students who complete high school requirements will have a marketable skill and can go directly to work in an entry-level position or continue their education at the community college. Upon completion of the AAS degree, students will have obtained competencies necessary to be hired at the master technician level. The students who wish to receive a four-year degree may transfer their AAS degree to an engineering technology program in a four-year university. Upon completion of the two additional years, a B.S. degree in engineering technology can be earned. This program also allows a high school student to meet all requirements for graduation and to enter a different college or university in a different field, if they change their career choice. In addition, an individual may pursue advanced education, return to work, and reenter education at any point.

Academic and Vocational Mix. The curriculum for this program is a blend of academics and vocational education that offers the student a chance for academic excellence and economic self-sufficiency through vocational education. The unique blending of the academic areas of mathematics and science with such vocational courses as power and transportation, basic technical drawing, and electronics produces a comprehensive curriculum that gives students a variety of education and career options.

Collaboration with Business, Industry, and Government. This collaborative agreement guarantees that the competencies identified within the curriculum are those that are actually required in the world of work.

With business representatives serving as consultants to the writing team, relevancy and accuracy of the curriculum are ensured. This unique collaboration in program planning and development is most essential for adequately preparing tomorrow's master technician.

Curriculum Framework

The Master Technician Program is made up of a series of courses that combines academic courses, especially in science and mathematics, with technology courses at the secondary level. The program also combines secondary and postsecondary courses at the community college to produce students with a higher level of skill and training. Specific secondary course requirements include two years of algebra, power and transportation, mechnical drawing, principles of technology, materials and processes, and electronics. Postsecondary courses include lasers and fiber optics, microwaves, communications, digital logic circuits, introduction to computers, fluid mechanics, robotics, instruments, and measurements. The courses have been carefully selected to provide students with a comprehensive background in complex systems, as opposed to the narrowly trained specialist.

Advantages of Master Technician Program

The Master Technician Program provides a broad knowledge base of academics and vocational education, with a solid background in the basics. It will produce a systems-oriented worker who will have attained academic excellence and economic self-sufficiency. A background in electronics provides many possibilities for a variety of job opportunities in such fields as telecommunications, automated manufacturing, systems analysis, biomedics, robotics, instrumentation controls, lasers, computer maintenance, fluid power, and fiber optics.

Business, industry, and the government have been involved from the inception of the program plan to insure that the competencies are indeed those needed in the field. In fact, business representatives have assured students that upon completion of this program jobs with opportunities for advancement will be available for them.

Future Projections

Educators as well as employers are excited about the cooperative effort in developing the Master Technician Program. The Peninsula's five secondary school divisions formally implemented the program at the ninth grade in the fall of 1986. However, some students in grades ten through twelve had also completed necessary program requirements to enter the program. Promotion of the new program took place during the 1985-86 school year in all area schools. Based upon the results of a Peninsula-wide survey in November 1986, over 400 students in grades nine through twelve indicated they were enrolled in one or more courses of the Master Technician Program.

Additional data will be gathered this school year to assist educators in making future predictions about students who complete the program. Interested students and parents see this Master Technician Program as an opportunity to be involved in the changing world of technology.

Virginia was faced with the challenge to provide for and benefit from new technology. Vocational-technical education in the state and in the nation will undergo a crucial test urging immediate and effective response to the sudden demands of a new technological society. The Master Technician Program is the Virginia Peninsula approach to accepting the challenges of new technology.

Doris K. Wimmer is assistant director for vocational education, Hampton City Schools, Virginia, and chairperson of the executive committee, Master Technician Program. She has previously served as a vocational curriculum specialist, supervisor of home economics, and home economics teacher for school divisions in the state of Virginia.

When a multicampus college writes articulation agreements with multiple public school systems, a particularly challenging enterprise is undertaken.

Merging Multiple Systems: Process and Problems

Eunice B. Kirkbride

A unique high school–community college articulation process has been developed in the metropolitan Washington, D.C. area of Northern Virginia. Leadership for this project has been provided by Northern Virginia Community College (NVCC), a multicampus institution, in cooperation with the public school systems in the nine jurisdictions that make up the constituency of the college. Northern Virginia Community College, the largest college in Virginia, has an enrollment of over 34,000 students. The supporting high schools have enrollments totaling nearly 100,000 students.

Articulation Defined

For our purposes, *articulation* is a planned process that coordinates instructional programs to enable student movement from high school to community college in related technical programs without duplicating previous coursework. The mechanism used to accomplish articulation is advanced placement.

Why Articulation?

Background. Some 80 percent of the program offerings at NVCC fall in the vocational-technical area. Each of the local jurisdictions also has strong programs in vocational education. Often the high school and college programs are related, with areas of overlap, providing potential and need for articulation.

The Northern Virginia area is growing rapidly, with heavy employment needs in the technology-dependent occupations and the service industries. Both the high schools and the community college offer programs to support these employment needs, which often, however, outstrip the supply.

Recently, the high schools emphasized increased graduation requirements in science and mathematics. While this emphasis is commendable, it also reduces opportunities in vocational education, since fewer hours are available for vocational electives. The outcome is that fewer students graduate from high school with adequate preparation for the work force. High school vocational students often do not see themselves as college bound and frequently do not make the move from high school to community college immediately, but generally flounder in low-paying jobs for a period of time.

Other students, well suited to vocational-technical education, are prevented from pursuing this avenue by parents who wish them to pursue baccalaureate education, regardless of the students' aptitude. Because of the nature of the highly educated community, parents and students often place great value on higher education, but they do not realize or appreciate the many excellent opportunities available at the technician level. These factors result in a severe shortage of skilled workers.

Beginnings. With these realities in mind, articulation efforts were initiated in December 1983, as a demonstration project, to determine if the largest college in the state could find a basis for articulation with the largest public school system in the state. An articulation plan, developed and signed in April 1984, described the process that has guided articulation efforts ever since. The purpose of the articulation project is to encourage strong vocational-technical programs. Competencies gained at the high school level are rewarded with appropriate advanced placement in the community college.

The project has been largely grant funded, with a series of Virginia Department of Education mini-grants and two Sears Partnership Development grants administered by the American Association of Community and Junior Colleges' (AACJC) Keeping America Working Project. The Virginia grants have supported the development of the original articulation plan and the writing of specific articulation agreements. The Sears/AACJC grants have supported a major regional conference to give wide visibility to the concept of articulation and the development of an implementation plan.

Students. The involved school districts share common problems. High school vocational education suffers from an unwarranted adverse image.

Some students are disinterested and poorly motivated. A great many more are bright, career oriented, and well motivated in their areas of special interest. Many lack accurate knowledge of the demands of the workplace and have naive ideas about life in the real world. Many are not motivated to pursue education beyond high school because of lack of knowledge about community college programs or lack of family support.

The community college teaches advanced versions of many programs taught in the high schools. Often the introductory material in a technical field at the college level duplicates or is similar to the material covered at the high school level. This duplicate instruction is wasteful of student time, human resources, and material assets, and students lose motivation when they are required to repeat previously learned competencies.

Goals and Purposes of Articulation

The underlying purpose of articulation is to provide recognition of excellence in technical education. This recognition of excellence is intended to encourage career-oriented students to continue their educations at the community college. With articulation, students with strong technical interests can be identified early, thus encouraging long-range planning. Further, to provide firsthand knowledge of the work world, students are encouraged by articulation to take advantage of the benefits of cooperative education.

Process of Articulation

Support. Administrative support for articulation at both the high school and the college has been vital to the progress of the project and has created a climate for the productive creativity of the committee members, who have written articulation agreements. In 1985 there were five agreements; in 1987 there were twenty-five agreements covering ten disciplines and all five campuses at NVCC.

Committees. Each articulation agreement is the work of a unique committee established to meet the needs of a specific discipline. The committees have experimented with various formats and have concluded that there is no ideal membership. Generally, the committees are composed of a coordinator, college faculty members, high school faculty members or curriculum specialists, and a college counselor assigned to the specific curriculum. This is not universally true, however. One committee was effective, and only one college faculty member and one high school vocational administrator were involved. The program is small and new in the high school, and there was a strong desire for students to have a career path in mind when the first high school class graduated in 1987. This is an example of the simplest form of articulation—one program, one campus, one school system.

More complex situations have also existed. One campus has two large school systems in its service area. Articulation agreements routinely require two sets of conditions to meet different circumstances in the two school systems. In this instance, committees are necessarily larger, with more intricate relationships.

Curricula. Both the high schools and the community colleges follow state curriculum guides in an attempt to achieve uniformity in the educational process. In truth, however, subtle and significant differences exist from one system to another. These differences are to be expected when institutions serve such widely different populations, although the differences create some problems in writing articulation agreements.

The first multicampus, multi-school system program to attempt articulation was Computer Information Systems. The committee that wrote the first agreement was composed of the program heads (who are also teaching faculty) from each campus, curriculum specialists from one large school system representing twenty-three high schools, the program counselor from one campus, the writer of a qualifying exam for the first course in the program, and the coordinator. The plan was to work out details with the one very large school system and then take the agreement to the other school systems for adaptation or acceptance. Curricula were compared and discussed, and basic decisions were made. It seemed as though articulation would be achieved fairly readily, since there was a good curriculum match.

ABLE Exams. The qualifying exam, Assessment by Local Examination (ABLE), was the vehicle to measure high school competency, so that advanced placement could be awarded. The ABLE exam is a teacher-made test designed to measure competency related to course objectives. Each question is matched to an objective, so that a comprehensive exam covers the entire content of the course. These ABLE exams exist in several areas. Students who performed well in the course were expected to test well on the examination, so that competency could be certified. The exam was administered to students on two campuses with the expected results.

The exam was then given to students in the large school system. The results were completely contrary to expectations. Disconcertingly, no clear correlation existed between course grades and grades on the ABLE exam, and only 19 percent of the high school students passed the exam. A complete item analysis of the exam showed certain questions to be extremely difficult for the students. These questions were examined and found to be valid. Most of them were clustered around a particular area of content. When the item analysis was discussed with the high school curriculum specialists and later with high school faculty members, it was learned that the troublesome area of content that received major attention in the college course was covered in the first year of the two-year high school program. The duplicated instruction may have contributed to the low pass rate on the ABLE exam.

Early in the winter of 1987, discussions with high school business division chairmen and faculty members clarified the expectations of the community college program. This open discussion of a thorny problem was productive. Faculty members at both levels were greatly concerned about the low pass rate and sought means to improve it in spring, 1987. Reviewing the NVCC Course Content Summary with high school faculty early enough in the year so that teachers could review the content with students and make the course objectives clear to students was an effective plan. Students knew that the ABLE exam questions measured the course objectives and came to the exam with a more serious attitude than seemed to be the case the first year. The results were gratifying. The pass rate on the exam increased by 37 percent, and the mean score on the exam rose ten points.

Because of the obstacles encountered, one campus and one school system are conducting a pilot study of the articulation agreement to solve the problems before implementing the agreement throughout the multicampus college and other school systems.

Complexities. The electronics agreement is the most complex articulation agreement to date. This agreement involves two campuses and four school systems. The four school systems include seventeen high schools with programs for students who have the full range of academic ability.

Some students in vocational programs lack sufficient self-confidence to pursue the high school math required as a prerequisite. The math deficiency created a stumbling block to articulation. Numerous meetings and discussions were held to resolve the issue: meetings and phone calls within and among the campuses, meetings with public school vocational administrators, and meetings with public school faculty members. Eventually, a solution emerged that maintained the principle that the high school math is a basic need for success in the program, and that advanced placement in the electronics courses is valid for a reasonable length of time to allow the student to correct any math deficiency through the college developmental math program.

The solution to the math problem demonstrates the importance of continuing to seek solutions to problems that arise so consensus can be reached. Creative problem solving and flexibility in addressing the issues allow for more viable articulation agreements. In this instance, the committee members made a concerted effort to reach an agreement that would be applicable to both campuses and to the four public school systems with electronics programs. It was difficult to achieve because of differences among programs, but a uniform agreement was deemed important by the committee; so a solution was found. The test will come when enough students from different jurisdictions enter the program with advanced placement so that valid comparisons can be made.

Differing Agreements. Another approach was employed for office systems technology. All campuses and all public school systems have popular programs in office systems technology and all five campuses have articulation agreements with the public school systems in their jurisdictions. One campus conducted a preliminary study, in which high school students were given ABLE exams in typing and shorthand, and their grades for the high school courses were compared with their grades on the ABLE exams. The level of high school competency required for advanced placement in the NVCC Office Systems Technologies Program was determined. Another campus and another school system adopted the same agreement without any changes. These agreements awarded seven college credits. Another campus and school system adopted an agreement that omitted shorthand and awarded six credits in typing. The campus that serves two school systems wrote an agreement with different conditions for each school system: one including typing and shorthand and the other including typing and word processing. Both these agreements awarded more credits than the other agreements.

These differences point out a difficulty in attempting to arrive at uniform agreements. Differences in emphasis and in student populations may mean that legitimate differences exist between programs, necessitating different agreements. If agreements differ, each campus must honor the other agreements, since students move freely among campuses. Agreements will be validated or revised, based on actual experience.

Long-Term Results

The only program with substantial experience in articulation is the nursing program, which has offered advanced placement to Licensed Practical Nurses (LPN) for seven years. This articulation is based on ABLE exams. Graduates of local high school LPN programs may take ABLE exams for the entire first year of nursing courses. The long-term history of articulation in this program had demonstrated that most LPNs can pass the first two ABLE exams, be assimilated with some special assistance into the generic nursing program, graduate, and pass the state licensing exam. The third ABLE exam has been in place for one year. Two students attempted this exam, but did not pass. Several more students will have the opportunity in 1987–88. Successful students may be exempt from courses worth twenty-three credits, a considerable saving in both time and money.

After some years of analyzing the results of LPN advanced placement, the nursing faculty determined that LPNs were weak in certain areas of content. Now a special course has been developed to guide the students' role transition. This successful articulation program has been monitored closely and the special needs of students have been met. Other programs now undertaking articulation will also need to monitor student progress and adapt their articulation measures accordingly.

Merging Cooperative Education

As experience in articulation was gained, the next logical extension of the project was to include cooperative education to provide curriculum-related work experience. A major problem for youth entering the work force is a lack of real world experience. The community college programs are heavy with required courses, allowing few, if any, electives. For cooperative education to succeed, therefore, students generally expand their programs over more than two years to allow time for the cooperative education component. Since cooperative education is not required in most technical programs in the college, it was not deemed justifiable to make cooperative education an integral part of the articulation agreements. However, cooperative education is highly recommended, and students are encouraged to enroll in cooperative education in addition to their technical programs. Excellent opportunities, which often lead to permanent employment, currently exist in cooperative education in Northern Virginia.

Faculty members readily see the benefits of experiential education. Young students, however, frequently need to be convinced that the time and effort involved in cooperative education will benefit them by increasing employment opportunities later. Students need strong incentives to enter the cooperative education program, and these incentives need to be explicit.

Factors That Aid Articulation

A number of factors have combined to aid articulation efforts. Strong statewide support exists for the effort, as evidenced by a joint resolution urging articulation signed by the president of the Virginia Board of Education and the chairman of the State Board for Community Colleges. Funding has been provided in the form of mini-grants to stimulate development of articulation agreements. The community college and the public school systems have provided release time for meetings. The individuals involved have given generously of their time and talent far beyond the release time provided and have conscientiously sought the common ground for articulation. People of good will have seen the potential student benefit and have prepared agreements that reward excellence and allow students a reasonable chance of success in the college programs.

Administrators and faculty members at both levels have expressed their desire to see students take advantage of articulation. High school educators are strongly supportive of postsecondary technical education and appreciate the advanced placement aspect of articulation. Advanced placement is a term well known to high school students; use of this term in relation to vocational education adds dignity and credibility to the program.

The most important aspect of the articulation process has been the emphasis on the "people process." In a few instances, articulation efforts have begun from adverse positions, which have arisen when people have not understood how to bring about the articulation or when some threat was perceived. In these cases, no progress was possible until the underlying problem was resolved. Fortunately, leaders of the curriculum coordinating committees were generally well prepared in group process or were amenable to suggestion.

Problems

Campus Versus College Orientation. Although currently the overall outcomes of articulation are decidedly positive, the process has not gone smoothly. Originally, the articulation project was seen as campus centered—each campus was to develop articulation agreements with the school districts in its local jurisdiction. This would be simple if students from a designated school district all attended a single campus of the college; however, students from any geographic location may, and do, attend any campus. Some programs are offered on every campus, while others are offered on only one or two campuses. Thus, there is a great need for collegewide coordination.

Testing Versus No Testing. Another problem area is the concept of advanced placement by testing for competency using an ABLE exam versus curriculum comparison without testing. Differences of opinion exist concerning placement testing. Faculty members in certain curricula feel that competency testing is essential to assure that graduates of the high school program have the same level of ability as those students who have taken the college course for which exemption is sought. Faculty members in other curricula feel that competency can be assured by comparing high school and community college course content. The ultimate goal is to eliminate ABLE exams by means of a predictor formula that will determine the level of high school proficiency required to predict success on the ABLE exam.

The ABLE exam process is somewhat cumbersome in preparation and administration, so a workshop was held in spring 1987, to help faculty members understand it. Faculty members working with nursing articulation have had extensive experience in using ABLE exams and find that the process is effective in predicting success in the nursing program. One special help course has been designed to aid LPN students, who enter with numerous credits of advanced placement, make the transition to RN student.

Increased Requirements for High School Diplomas. In Virginia the high school diploma, which previously required eighteen units of education, now requires twenty; the prestigious Governor's Diploma requires twenty-two. More emphasis is now placed on math and science, an emphasis expected to provide better-prepared students. Changed emphasis in the high school programs may affect vocational students, however, because less time is available for vocational electives. Most vocational students do not opt for the Governor's Diploma, so this impact is not clear yet.

Calendar Change. An unforeseen complexity entered the picture when a major change in the Virginia Community College System calendar was advanced by one year. A change from the quarter system to the semester system is due to take effect in the summer of 1988, which has necessitated major revisions in all college curricula and student record keeping. Since in many cases the same people who have been involved in articulation are also involved in the semester conversion, severe time constraints have limited articulation efforts somewhat. In most instances, however, people have extended themselves to accomplish both articulation and semester conversion.

Cross-Campus Coordination. The issue of campus orientation versus collegewide orientation (previously mentioned) has been difficult to address because the problem does not lend itself to a simple solution. While NVCC is a multicampus college, it is also one college with students moving freely between campuses. Campus autonomy has been an important concept for a long time; yet intercampus coordination of multicampus programs is becoming a more important issue because of intercampus transfers. A cross-campus coordinating group, composed of representatives from each campus, has tried to promote a collegewide view of articulation. Developed primarily for information sharing, the group has neither a clear-cut charge nor clear lines of responsibility or authority. Therefore, while the group carries the potential for finding solutions, it has not developed as a problem-solving body and thus far has been relatively ineffective. The function of this body remains an issue to be resolved. At the present time, intercampus coordination is in the hands of the dean of academic and student services, who holds overall responsibility for the entire project.

Outcomes

Good Will. The greatest aid to resolution of the problems that have arisen has been the exceptionally strong good will of the people involved in this project. From the beginning, the focus has been on the welfare of the students. The overriding concern about what is best for the student encouraged people to put aside personal interests and to focus on developing articulation agreements that provide the most supportive academic climate for student success.

Administrative Involvement. Administrative support for articulation efforts, outstanding at both the college and secondary school levels, has been vital to the success of the project, especially as problems have been encountered. Administrators have been actively involved throughout the life of the project with firsthand knowledge of the difficulties and have made significant contributions to problem resolutions.

Support Groups. New support groups have developed between high school and college personnel. A number of committees have been formed that have resulted in greatly improved communication between related groups. On the two largest campuses, steering committees guide and oversee the articulation process. The curricular committees, small, ongoing committees formed at the teaching level, share information and develop functional articulation agreements. Members are usually faculty members, curriculum specialists, and counselors associated with a particular discipline. Once an articulation agreement is signed, the curricular committee will continue to meet, at least annually, to monitor the effect of the agreement and propose revisions as necessary. Thus, a vital communication link is forged, resulting in much improved understanding of program expectations at both levels. No longer is it necessary to speak in the abstract about high school and college. Faces and phone numbers are known and direct communication takes place.

Summary

The purpose of the articulation project in Northern Virginia is to enhance and encourage strong vocational-technical programs by certifying competencies gained at the high school level and rewarding such competency with appropriate advanced placement in the community college. This purpose has been achieved in ten curricular areas, some representing programs on multiple campuses. A small number of students have already been admitted to the college with advanced placement in technical programs, and more students are expected each year.

The next step in articulation will be to make junior high and high school students and their parents more fully aware of the opportunities available through vocational-technical education. Students will be encouraged to begin career planning early and to take advantage of the benefits of articulation and cooperative education.

The major elements of the articulation process are (1) a clear, comprehensive plan, (2) good communication among participants, (3) strong administrative support at both levels, (4) unity toward a common purpose, (5) focus on academically sound procedures to assure students a reasonable chance for success, (6) emphasis on long-range career planning.

Good will and open communication have characterized the project from the beginning and remain the basic building blocks for future development and implementation. Freedom to experiment with various methods for achieving articulation has been a hallmark of the project and has contributed to the viability of the program. While following the general guidelines of the plan, each faculty group has worked out the details according to the demands of the programs, always keeping in mind the best interests of the student. As problems have arisen, creative solutions have been sought, so that a flexible program has emerged with provision for periodic revision and review.

Although still in a process of development, articulation has proven to be a workable concept for strengthening technical education in Northern Virginia.

Eunice B. Kirkbride is director of the NVCC Keeping America Working Project and a professor of nursing. She is author of the plan for articulation between Northern Virginia Community College and its high school constituencies.

Index

A

Academic classes, sequencing of, 42-43
Academic rank, in high school, 76, 77
Advanced placement, 16, 73, 93; at Northern Virginia Community College, 101, 102, 104-106, 108-109, 110
Advanced Placement (AP) Examination, 13-14, 19, 21
American Association of Community and Junior Colleges (AACJC), 29, 30, 102
America Association for Higher Education, 71, 83
American Ballet Theater II, 89
American Council on Education, 19
Arizona, 61-67
Aronson, R., 71, 83
Articulation, concept of, 101-111. *See also* Collaboration, high school-college
Asian youth, 41, 76
Assessment by Local Examination (ABLE), 104-105, 106, 108-109
Associate in Applied Science (AAS) degree, 96, 98
Association of College and Secondary Schools of the Middle States and Maryland, 16-17
At-risk students, 5, 7-10, 30-32; community colleges and, 51-59, 61-67; at Middle College High School, 40-46, 74
Attendance rate, 38, 41-42, 46

B

Basic skills, 21, 20, 43-44, 45, 55-57, 62
Bentley-Baker, K., 86
Berman, P., 71, 83
Black youth, 7, 85; at-risk, 28-29, 31; college education and, 19, 72; at Middle College High School; 41, 76

Blanchard, B. E., 73, 83
Bouton, C., 53, 54-55, 59
Boyer, E. L., 15, 20, 22, 69, 72, 82, 83
Brawer, F. B., 56, 59
Bronx Community College, 48
Brooklyn College, 48
Brubacher, J. S., 15, 17, 22
Bruffee, K. A., 53, 55, 59
Business Advisory Commission, 7, 11, 30, 31, 32
Butler, N. M., 16

C

CAL-Arts, 89
California, 13, 15, 20
California Achievement Tests, 76, 81, 82
Career education programs, 38, 42-44, 57-59, 76, 107
Carlson, R., 71, 83
Carnegie Corporation, 38
Carnegie Forum, 5, 20
Center for Excellence, 90
Chapman, D. W., 70, 84
Chickering, A. W., 54, 59
Childbearing age, 8
City-As-School High School, 74, 75, 84
City-As-School (CAS) program, 70, 74-82
City University Board of Trustees, 45
City University of New York, 38, 48, 74
Civil rights movement, 6, 27
Clark, T. A., 19, 22
Clinical experience, in community colleges, 57, 58
Cohen, A. M., 56, 59
Cold War, 6
Collaboration, with business, 5, 96-100
Collaboration, high school-college, 5, 9-10, 14-22, 48. *See also* Concurrent enrollment programs
Collaborative learning, 53-55

113

College Entrance Examination Board, 16-17
College Now program, 70, 74-82
College Orientation Program, 61-68
College-School Collaboration: Appraising the Major Approaches, 1
Columbia University, 15, 16
Commission for the Reorganization of Secondary Education, 17
Committee of Ten, 16, 17
Community colleges, 26-27, 28, 32; advanced placement at, 98, 99, 101-110; at-risk students at, 51-59, 61-67; collaboration at, 48, 72, 75. *See also specific community colleges*
Commuter students, 53
Competition, international, 6, 18
Concurrent enrollment programs, 16, 44-45, 70-83, 86-93, 101-110
Consumer Price Index, 73
Cooperative education programs, 38, 42-44, 57-59, 76, 107
Cooperative Institutional Research Program (CIRP), 79
Coping skills, 63-64
Cullen, C., 37-49
CUNY Freshman Skills Assessment Tests, 45, 75
Curriculum redundancy, 45, 73, 103, 104-105

D

Dade County Public Schools (DCPS), 85, 86-87, 88-89, 90, 92
D'Agostino, R., 98
Daly, W. T., 1
de Lancie, J., 93
Delta College, 53
Disabled adults, 30
Disconnecting, phenomenon of, 7
Displaced homemakers, 30
Dougherty Foundation, 66
Dropout rate, 30; in American schools, 7-8, 18, 21, 28-29, 71; at Middle College High School, 37, 38, 44, 48, 74, 75
Dual enrollment programs. *See* Concurrent enrollment programs
Duley, J. S., 57, 60
Dumbauld, E., 32

E

Eastern United States, 15, 16, 71, 72, 97, 101-111
Eastman School of Music, 89
Economically disadvantaged youth. *See* Low-income youth
Education Commission of the States (ECS), 7, 8, 9, 30, 31
Educational Testing Service, 14
Elderly, 30
Elementary education, 7, 10, 14, 15, 26
Eliot, President (Harvard), 16
Elsbree, L., 53, 60
Emphasis on Excellence program, 86
English-as-a-second-language programs, 62
Evergreen College, 53
Externships, 57
Extracurricular activities, 44

F

Faculty development programs, 21-22, 44, 56
Failure cycle, for at-risk youth, 8-9, 13
Family structure, failure of, 8-9
Flemming, A., 30, 32
Flood gate principle, 71
Florida, 71, 72, 85-93
Florida International University (FIU), 90, 92
Florida Legislature, 86, 90
Ford Foundation, 10, 19, 48, 62, 66
Fund for the Improvement of Postsecondary Education, 38

G

Gamson, Z. F., 54, 59
Garfield High School, 13, 14, 21
Garth, R. Y., 53, 54-55, 59
GI Bill (1944), 17, 26, 27
Gifted programs, 85, 86
Gifted students. *See* High-achieving students
Gollattscheck, J. F., 25-33
Goodlad, J. I., 5, 11
Governor's Diploma, Virginia, 109
Grade average, high school, 76, 77, 79-82

Grade point average (GPA), 79-82
Graduation rate, 19, 21
Graham, J., 55, 60
Great Depression, 17
Greenberg, A. R., 69-84
Group counseling, 38, 46-47
Gymnasium, German model of, 15

H

Hagen, U., 87
Hall, E. B., 18
Hampton, school division of, 96, 99-100
Hanson, D., 87
Harlacher, E. L., 32
Harper, W., 16
Harry S. Truman Lecture, 30
Harvard University, 15, 16, 26
Hendrickson, A. D., 71, 84
High-achieving students, 8, 69, 75, 82-83, 85, 86
High-risk students. *See* At-risk students
High School and Beyond Survey, 28
High School teacher institutes, 18
Higher education, 10-11, 26-27
Higher Education Research Institute, 72-84
Hill, S. A., 14, 22
Hispanic Policy Development Project, 28
Hispanic youth, 7, 85; at-risk, 8, 28, 31; college education and, 13, 14, 19; at Middle College High School, 41, 76
Hoffman, M. S., 26, 32
Homework, 6
Honig, W., 20
Hostos, Community College, 48
Howard University, 89

I

Illinois, 48
Illiteracy, adult, 29-30
Immigrants, 30, 48
Integration, of schools, 27, 85-86
Interdisciplinarity, 56
Internship preparation courses, 43
Internships, 42-44, 47, 57, 58

J

Japan, 7, 14, 20
Janaro, R., 86
Job production, in United States, 7
Johns Hopkins University, 75
Johnston, W. B., 32
Junior colleges, 28, 32

K

Katz, J., 53, 60
Kearns, D., 29
Keeping America Working Project, 102
Keeping Students in School, 28-29, 33
Kent, A., 87
Kingsborough Community College, 74-75
Kirkbride, E. B., 57, 101-111
Klein, K., 91
Kleinrock, K. J., 70, 84

L

LaGuardia Community College, 5, 18-19, 48; collaboration at, 14, 38-40, 42, 44-46, 74; as model, 9, 11, 47, 76
Land-Grant Colleges Act (1862), 26, 27
Language skills, 18, 64
Learning communities, 53-55
Learning groups, 53-54
Learning in Groups, 53, 59
Lesley College, 53
Lewis, D., 93
Lieberman, J., 38, 75, 76, 84
Literacy rate, 10
Logan, J., 87
Love, E., 93
Low-achieving students, 69, 70-73, 75, 76-83
Low-income youth, 29, 31, 73; in College Orientation Program, 61, 62, 66; at Middle College High School, 41, 76

M

McCabe, R., 93
McCartan, A. M., 51-60

McMaster University, 53
Maguire, N. D., 71, 84
Maimon, E. P., 53, 55, 60
Massachusetts Teachers Association, 16
Master Technician Program, 95-100
Mathematics skills, 14, 20, 21; in College Orientation Program, 64; at Middle College High School, 41, 44, 75; at North Virginia Community College, 102, 105, 109
Matthews, J., 13, 23
Meredith, J., 27
Miami-Dade Community College (MDCC), 86-89, 90, 91, 92, 93
Michigan, 15
Micro-counseling techniques, 47
Middle College High School, 9, 11, 21; at-risk students at, 18-19, 37-48, 75-79, 81-82; collaboration at, 10, 14, 70, 74
Middle-income families, 73
Minnesota, 71, 72, 74, 84
Minority students, 5, 7, 27, 85; at-risk, 8, 28-30, 31; college education and, 13, 14, 19, 72; in College Orientation Program, 61, 62, 66; at Middle College High School, 41, 76
Moderate-achieving students, 70-73, 75, 77-83
Moed, M. G., 37-49
Morrill Act (1862), 26, 27
Morris, M., 14, 23
Muller, K., 85-93

N

National Academy of Science, 20
National Aeronautics and Space Administration (NASA), 6, 97
National Assessment of Educational Progress, 6
National Association of Secondary School Principals, 71, 83
National Association for State Universities and Land Grant Colleges, 19
National Defense Education Act, 18
National Education Association (NEA), 16, 17
National Endowment for the Humanities, 19, 22
National Foundation for the Advancement of the Arts, 89
National Governors Association, 5
National Research Council, 14
National Science Foundation, 22
New England's First Fruits, 26, 32
New Horizons Technical Center, 96
New Jersey, 48
New World School of the Arts (NWSA), 85, 90, 91-93
New York City, 37-38, 48, 73, 74-75
New York City Board of Education, 38, 39, 74, 75
N.Y.C. Tests in Reading and Mathematics, 45
New York State, 16, 71, 72
N.Y.S. Regents Competency Tests, 15-16, 45
New York State Legislature, 48
New York State colleges, 48
New York Times, 41
New York University (NYU), 89
Newman, F., 5-11
Newport News, school division of, 96, 99-100
Newport News Shipbuilding, 97
North Carolna National Bank, 90
North Carolina School of the Arts, 89
North Central United States, 15, 29, 48
North Virginia Community College (NVCC), 101-111
Northeastern United States, 29
Northwest Ordinance, 27
Northwestern Senior High School, 85-86

O

Office of the State Course Numbering System (Florida), 87
Oklahoma, 71, 74
Open-door policy, 17, 27
Opportunity for all, concept of, 25-32
Ordovensky, P., 29, 32
Orientation for Student Development, 63
Orr, M. T., 28-29, 33
Osborn, J. W., 73, 84
Osborne, K. Q., 53, 60

P

Packer, A. E., 32
Parental support groups, 47
Parsons Institute, 89
Peer counseling, 38, 47
Peer support groups, 53, 54
Pelton, M., 86
Performing and Visual Arts Center (PAVAC), 85-90, 92
Phillips, C. G., 98
Phillips Academy of Andover, 16
Poquoson, school division of, 96, 99-100
Pratt Institute, 89
Pregnancy, teenage, 8
Preparatory schools, 15, 16, 17
President's Commission on Higher Education (1946), 27
Princeton University, 15
Project Advance, 75, 83
Public school education, 26-28

R

Ramist, L., 69, 72, 84
Randall, R., 71, 84
Reading skills, 10, 41, 44, 55-56, 64, 75
Reconnecting Youth: The Next Stage of Reform, 7, 11, 30, 32
Refugees, 30
Remediation, 21, 43, 44, 56, 75
Rice, B., 54, 59
Robb, C. M., 96
Roberts, E., 32
Rockefeller Foundation, 22
Rothman, R., 69, 72, 84
Rudolph, F., 16, 23

S

St. Mary's High School, 62
Sarah Lawrence College, 89
Sarmiento, M., 85, 86
Scholastic Aptitude Tests (SAT), 6, 76, 78, 81
Science skills, 18, 21, 102, 109
Sears Partnership Development Grant, 102
Secondary education, 7, 10, 13-22. See also *specific programs*
Secondary/Postsecondary Program to Prepare Master Technicians, 97
Segregation, racial, 27
Self-esteem, among at-risk students, 9
Seminole Community College, 84
Seminole County School Board, 71, 84
Sequenced education program, 20, 42-43
Service industry jobs, 31, 70
Servicemen's Readjustment Act (1944), 26
Sexton, P. C., 72, 84
Sexton, R. F., 57, 60
Sherman, D., 56-57, 60
Simms, R. B., 52, 60
Simon's Rock Early College, 18
Single-parent families, 8, 30, 41
Sizer, T. R., 5, 11
Skills-across-the-curriculum program, 55-56
Skills assessment, 64
Smith, B. L., 55, 60
South Florida School of the Arts, 90
South Mountain Community College, 61, 62, 67
Southern United States, 28, 48. See also *Florida*
Spring Hill Gathering (1987), 22
Sputnik crisis, 18
Stoel, C. F., 13-23
Structured Employment/Economic Development Corporation, 28
Student development programs, 54
Student government, 47
Student-as-worker, ethic of, 38
Study groups, 53, 54
Study skills, 63
SUNY College, 53
Syracuse University, 75, 83

T

Taylor, C., 56-57, 60
Teacher certification, 6
Teacher development, 21-22, 44, 56
Team teaching, 56-57
Technical colleges, 28, 32
Tennessee, 48
Test scores, 6, 10, 21, 64; minorities and, 7, 29, 76

Testing, of students, 6, 17, 21; advanced placement and, 104, 106, 108; in alternative programs, 45, 64, 87. *See also specific tests*
Testing, of teacher candidates, 6
Textbooks, 20
Thomas Nelson Community College, 96, 98
Three-Year Collegiate Program, 75
Transfer Opportunities Program, 62
Truman, H., 27
Two-plus-two program, 95-96, 98

U

Unemployment, 7, 30, 31
Ungerer, R. A., 57, 60
United States, 7, 8, 14, 20, 25-32, 69. *See also specific states.*
U.S. Bureau of the Census, 73, 84
U.S. Bureau of Labor Statistics, 73
U.S. Congress, 22
U.S. Constitution, 25-26, 27
U.S. Department of Education, 1
U.S. Department of Labor, 31, 97
U.S. Supreme Court, 27
Universal education, 17, 25-32
University of California (Los Angeles), 79
University of Chicago, 16
University of Miami, 90
University of Michigan, 15
University of Mississippi, 27
Upper-income families, 8, 29
Upward Bound, 18
Upward mobility, 71
Urban youth, 13, 28, 29, 37
USA Today, 29, 32

V

van Aalst, F. D., 59, 60
Vaughan, G. B., 27, 33
Villella, E., 87
Virginia Board of Education, 107
Virginia Community College System, 96, 109
Virginia Department of Education, 96, 102
Virginia Peninsula, 96, 97, 99-100
Virginia Peninsula Vocational Training Council (VPVTC), 96-97
Virginia State Board for Community Colleges, 107
Virginia State Board of Education, 96
Vocational-technical programs, 57, 95-111
von Braun, W., 6

W

Warren, E. A., 61, 67
Washington, D.C., 9, 101
Washington Post, 13, 14
Weekend Learning Community, 53
Wehrwein, A. C., 71, 84
Weiss, A., 91
Western Europe, 7
Western United States, 13, 15, 20, 28
What to Do About Youth Dropouts?, 28
White, A. M., 56, 60
White youth, 7, 8, 85; dropout rate among, 28, 29; at Middle College High School, 41, 76
Wilbur, F. P., 70, 84
Williamsburg/James City County, school division of, 96, 99-100
Willingham, W., 14, 23
Willis, R., 15, 17, 22
Wilson, R., 19, 23
Wilson, R. C., 54, 60
Wimmer, D. K., 95-100
Work experience programs, 38, 42-44, 57-59, 76, 107
Work groups, 53
World War II, 17
Writing skills, 55, 56, 75
Wygal, B. R., 32

Y

Yale New Haven Institute, 19, 22
Yale University, 15, 19
York County, school division of, 96, 99-100